THE ART OF MINDFULNESS

JOYFUL AND RADIANT COLOURING

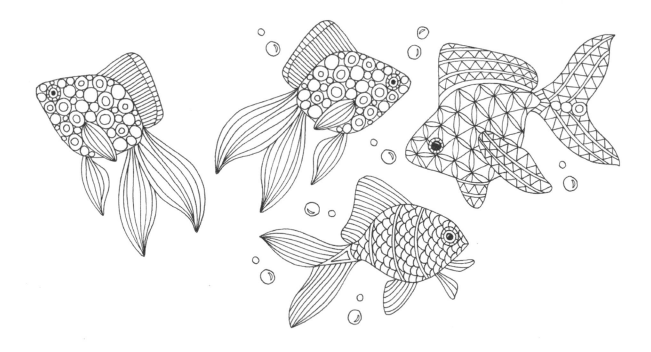

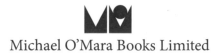

Michael O'Mara Books Limited

First published in Great Britain in 2016 by
Michael O'Mara Books Limited
9 Lion Yard
Tremadoc Road
London SW4 7NQ

A CIP catalogue record for this book is available from the British Library.

Papers used by Michael O'Mara Books Limited are natural, recyclable products made from wood grown in sustainable forests. The manufacturing processes conform to the environmental regulations of the country of origin.

ISBN: 978-1-78243-630-0

2 3 4 5 6 7 8 9 10

www.mombooks.com

Designed by Ana Bjezancevic and Claire Cater

Illustrations by Elisé Gilbert, Emily Hamilton, Gavin Rutherford, Jake McDonald, Jasmine Burgess, Jo Taylor, Julie Ingham, Kay Widdowson, Lizzie Preston, Louise Wright and Maxime Lebrun

Cover illustration by Lizzie Preston

Printed and bound in Germany

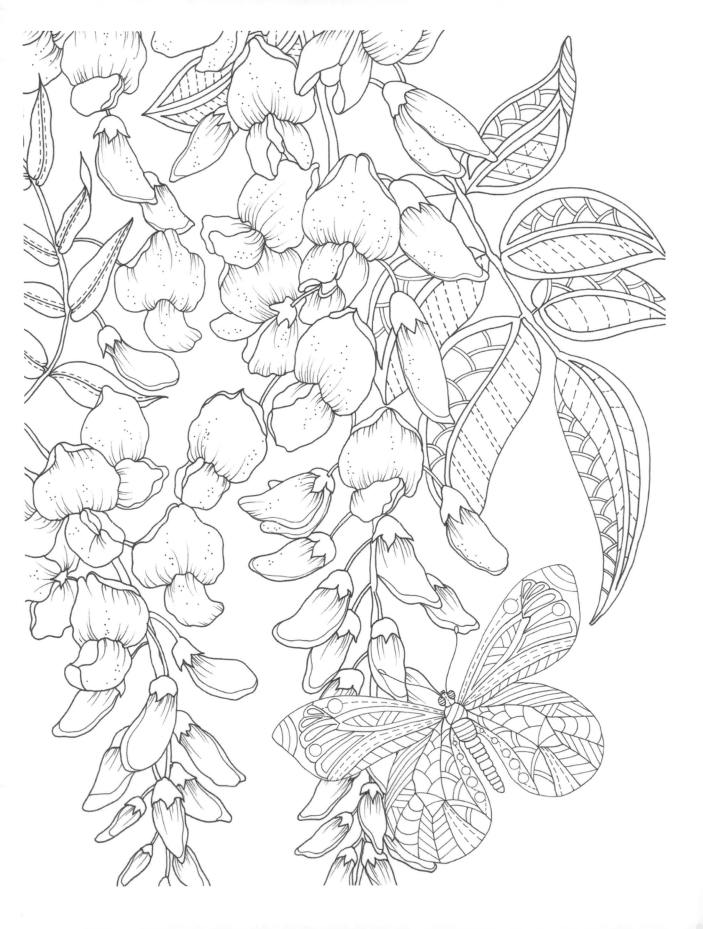

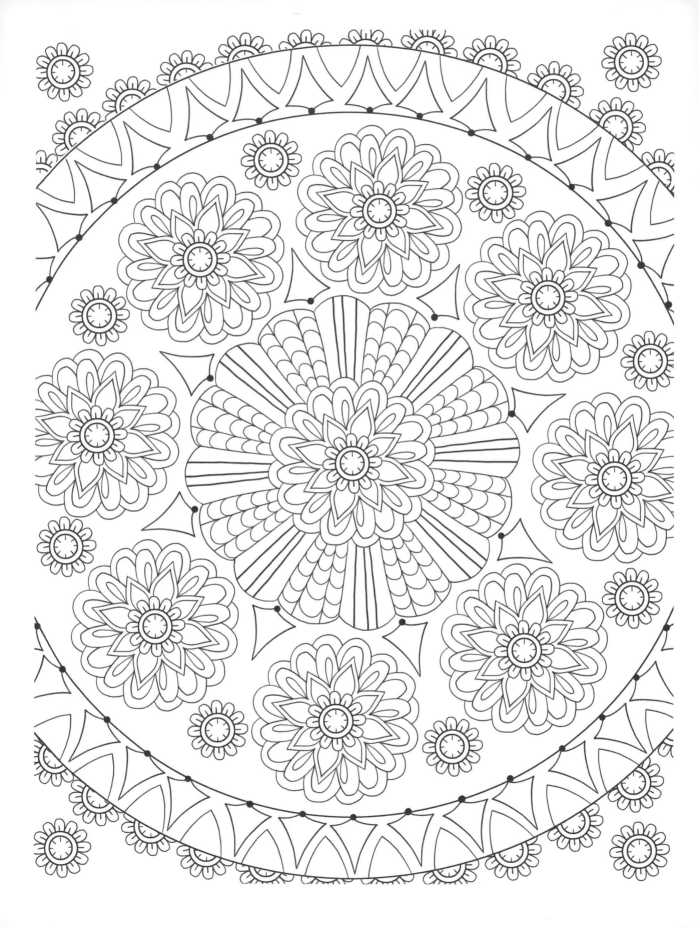

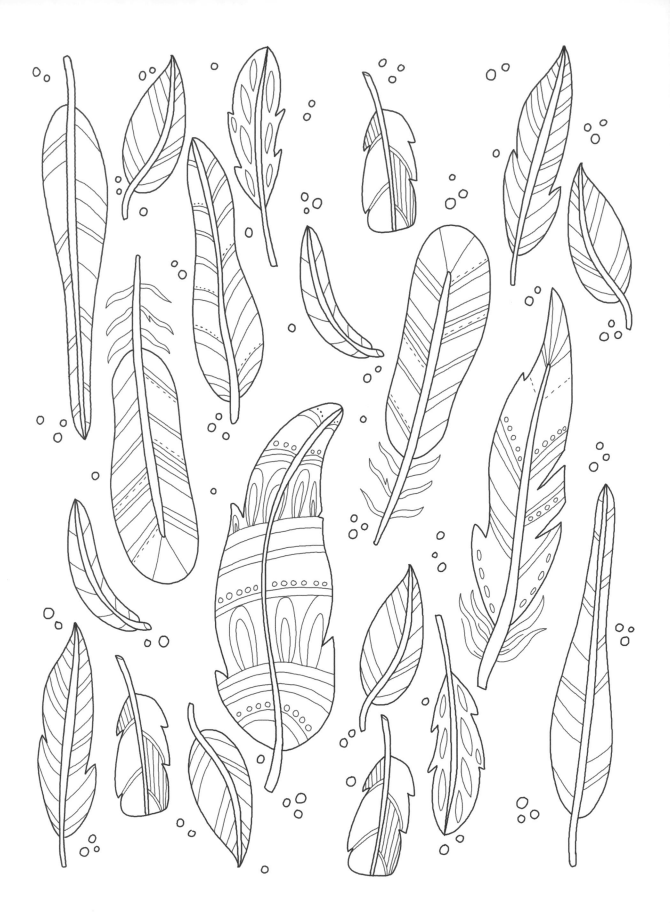

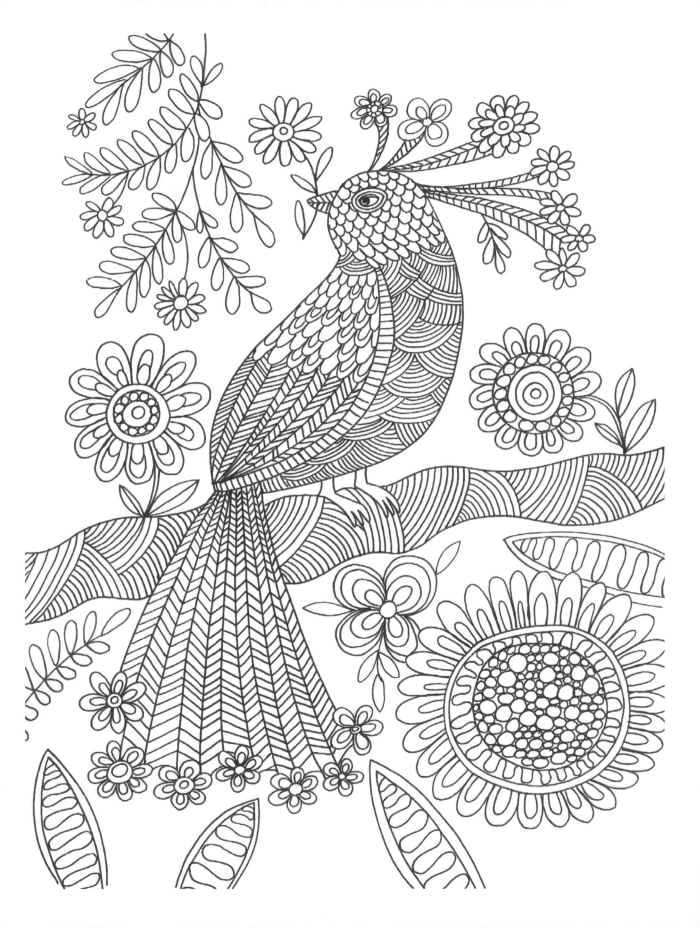

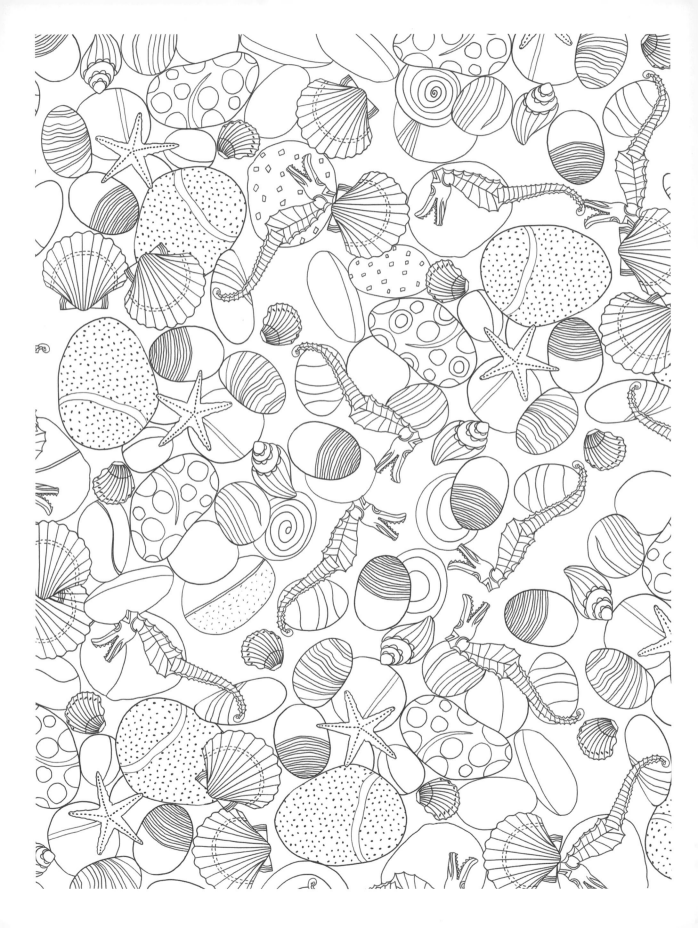

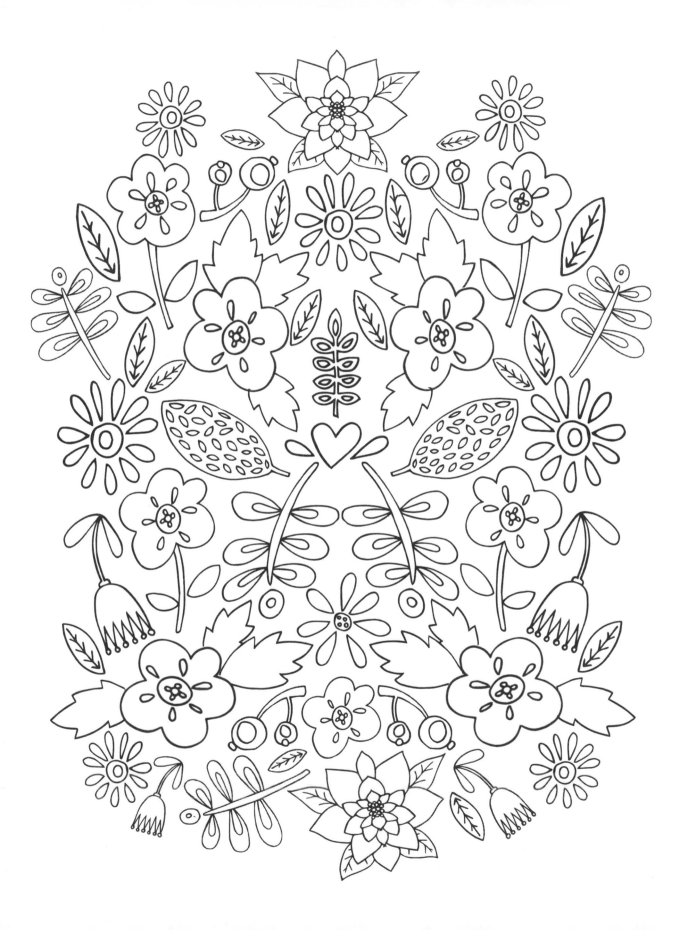

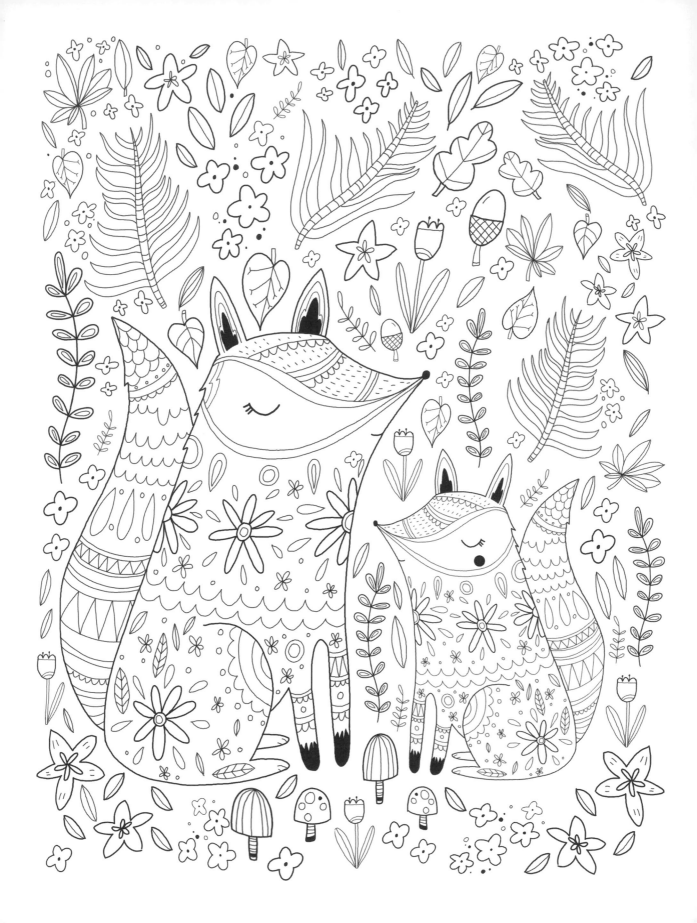

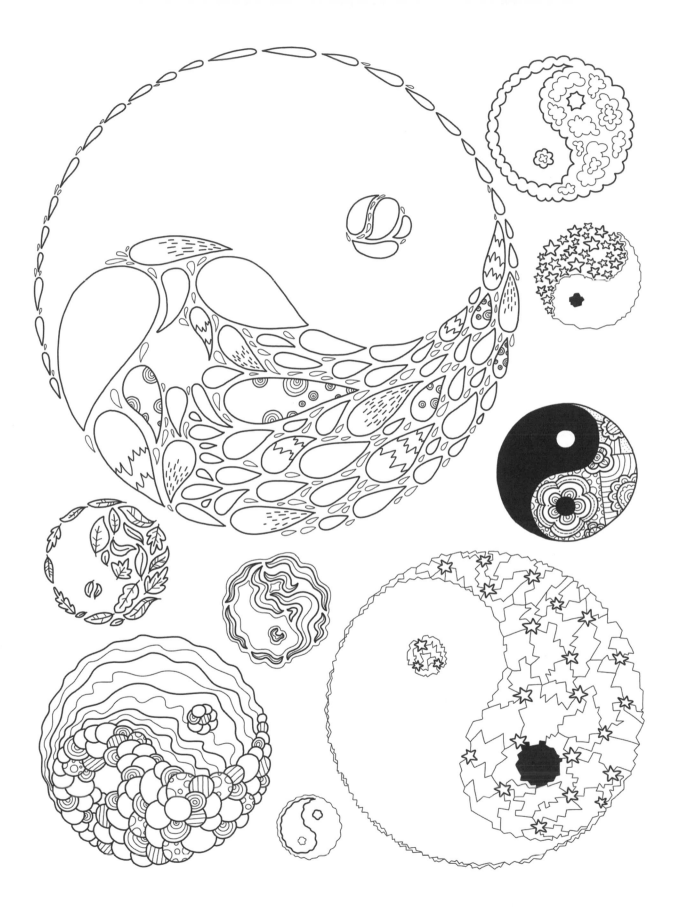

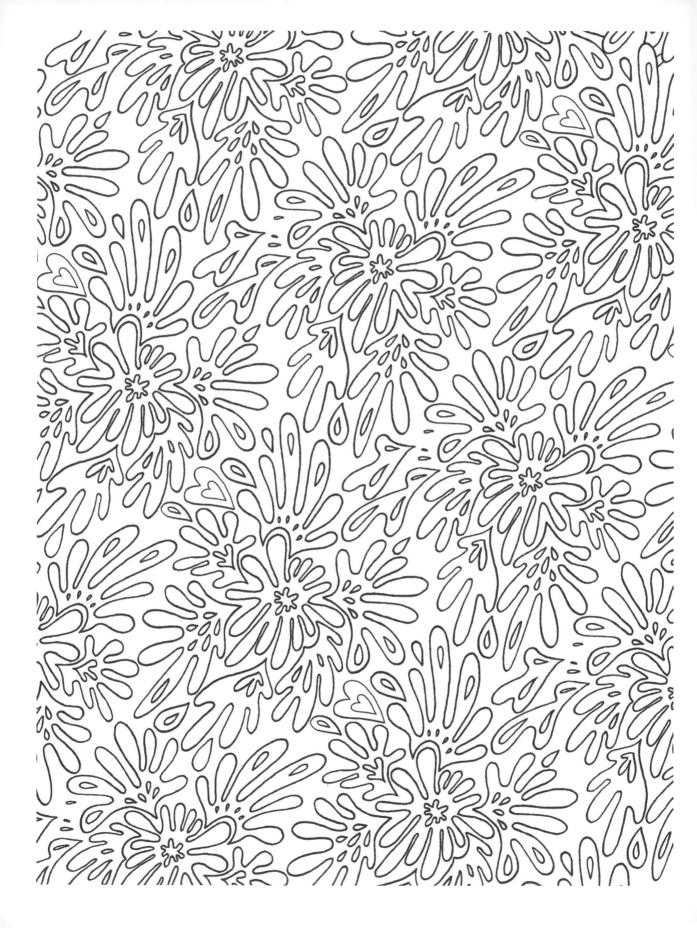

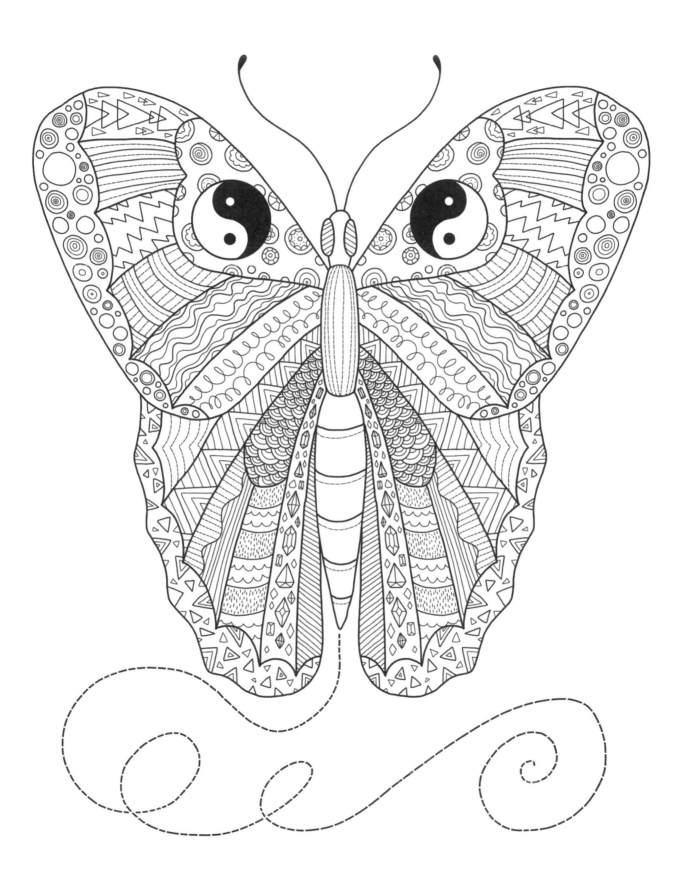

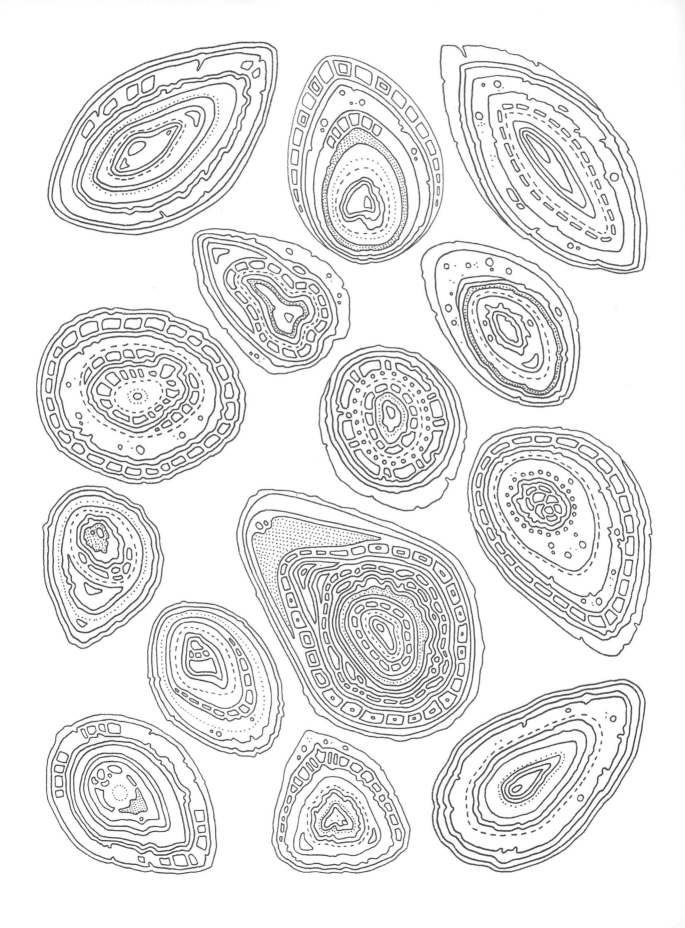

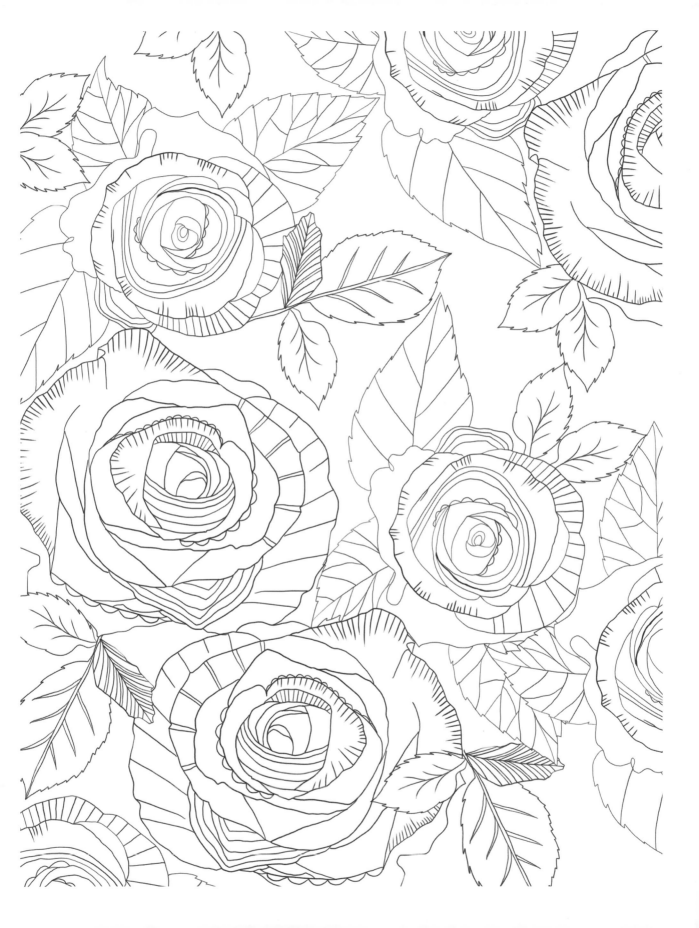

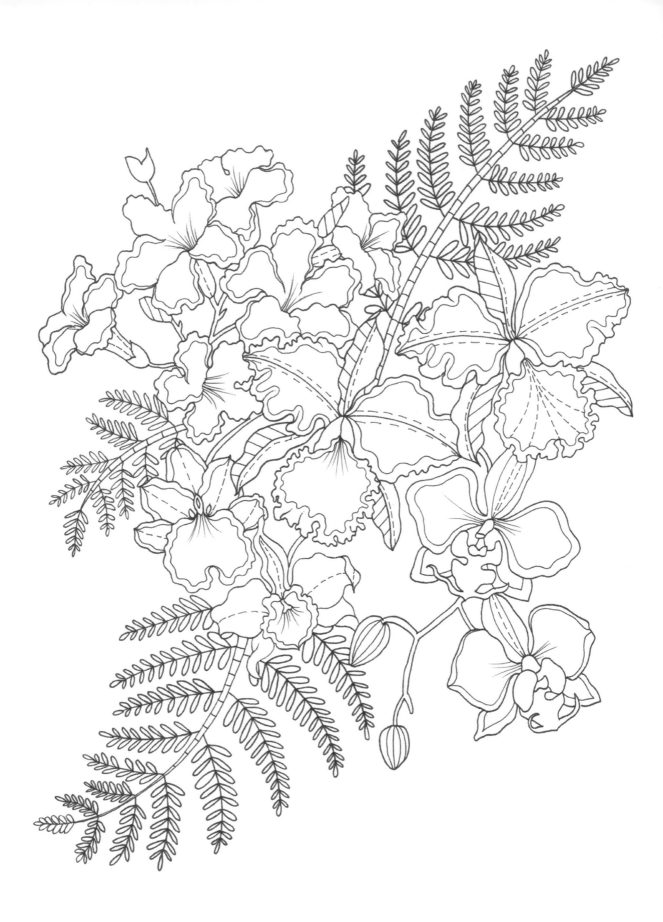

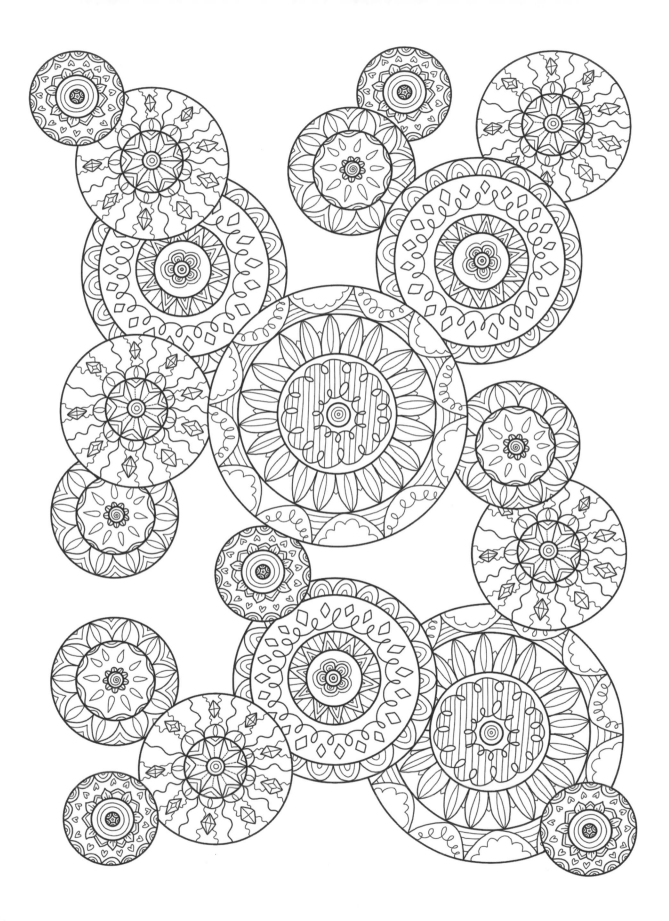

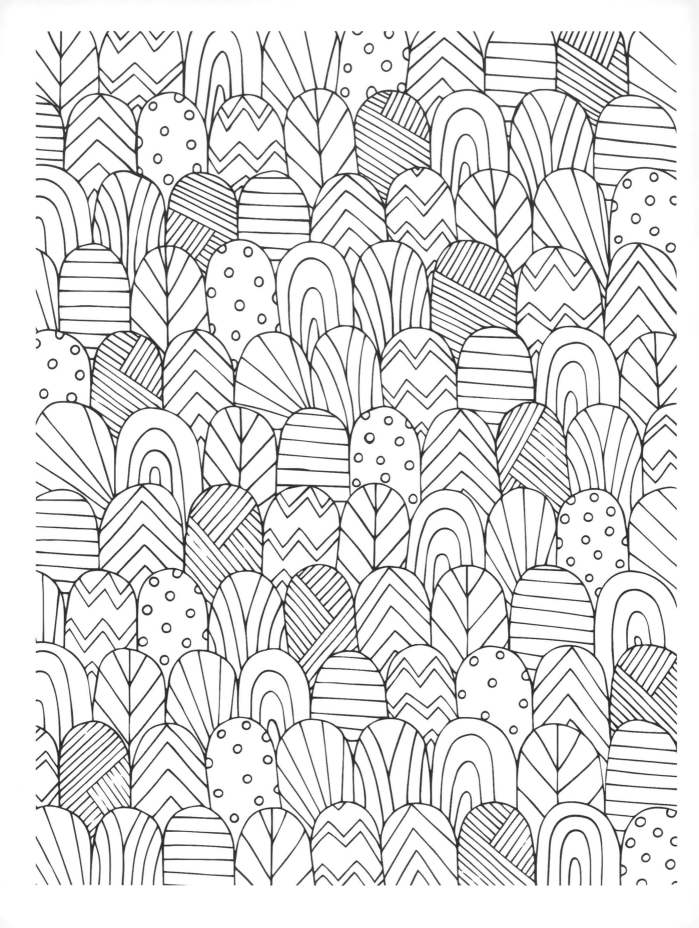

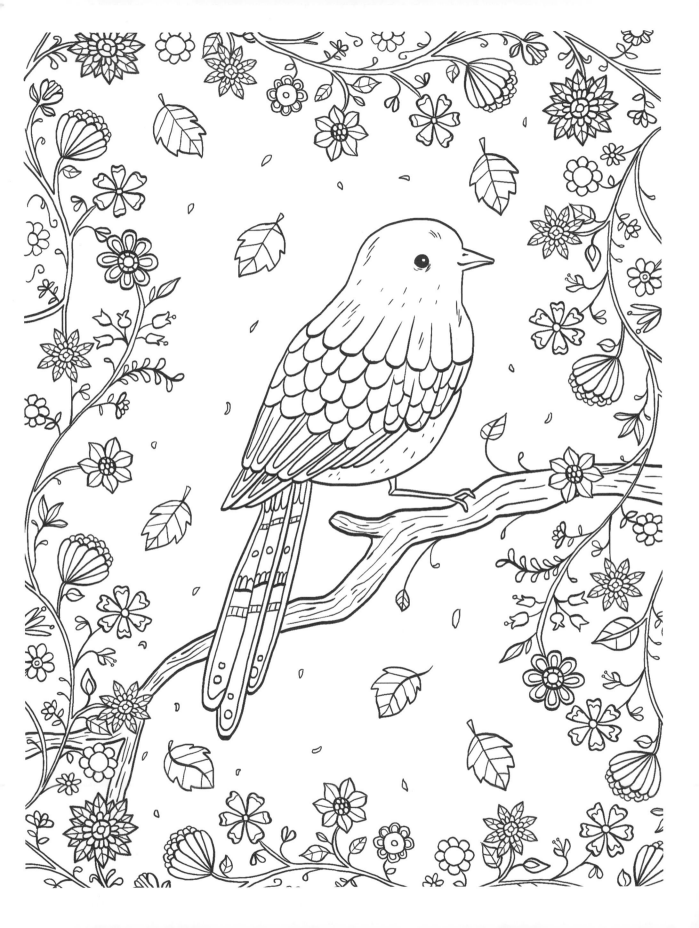

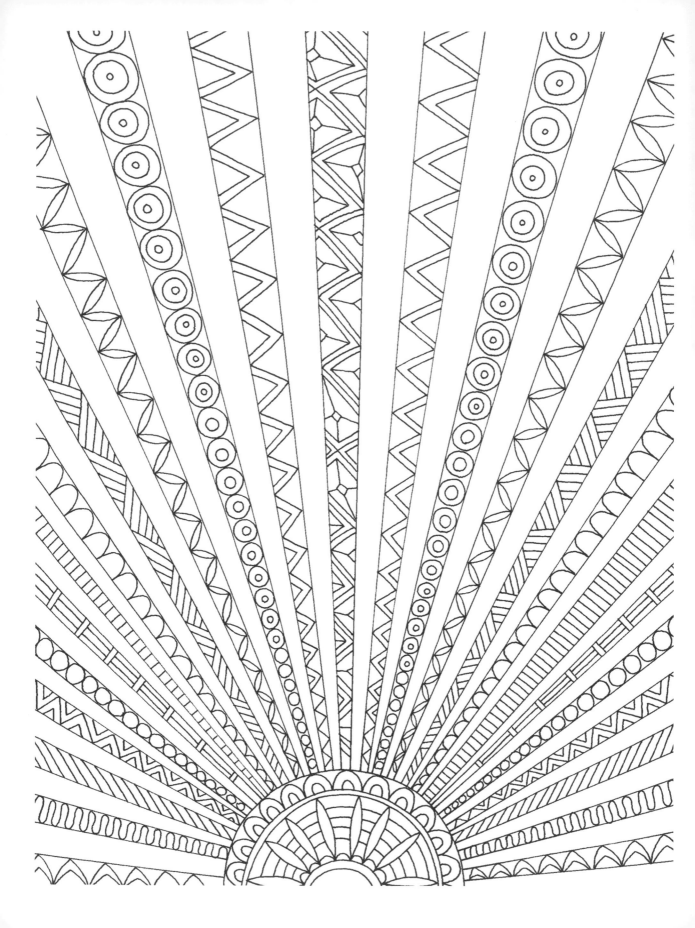

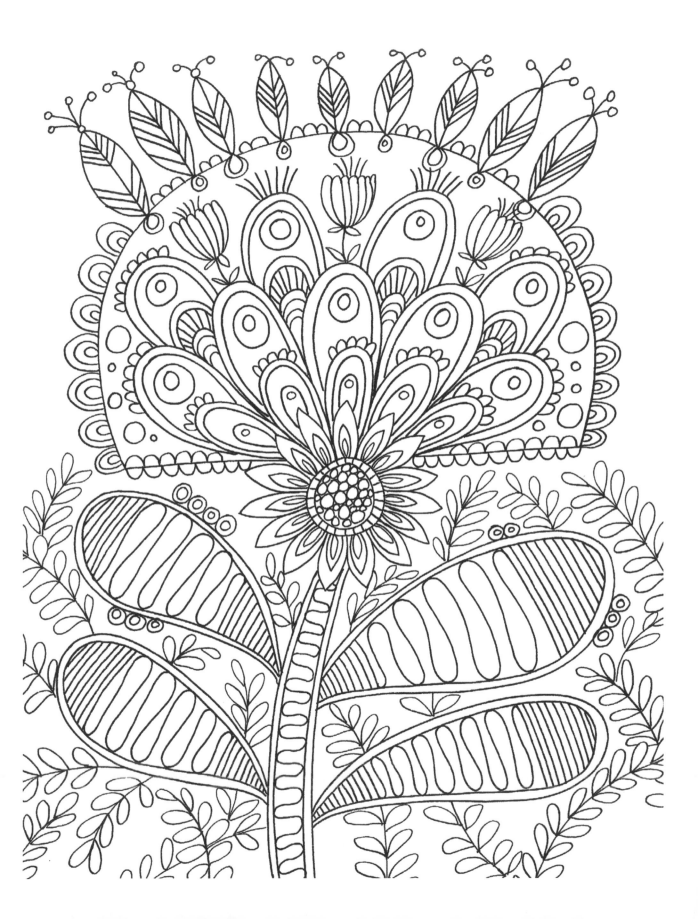

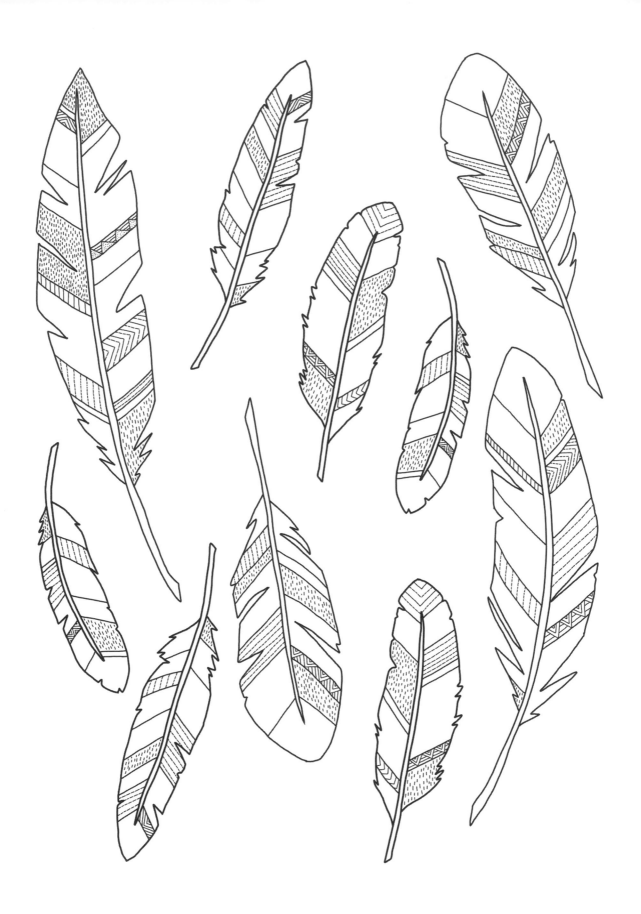

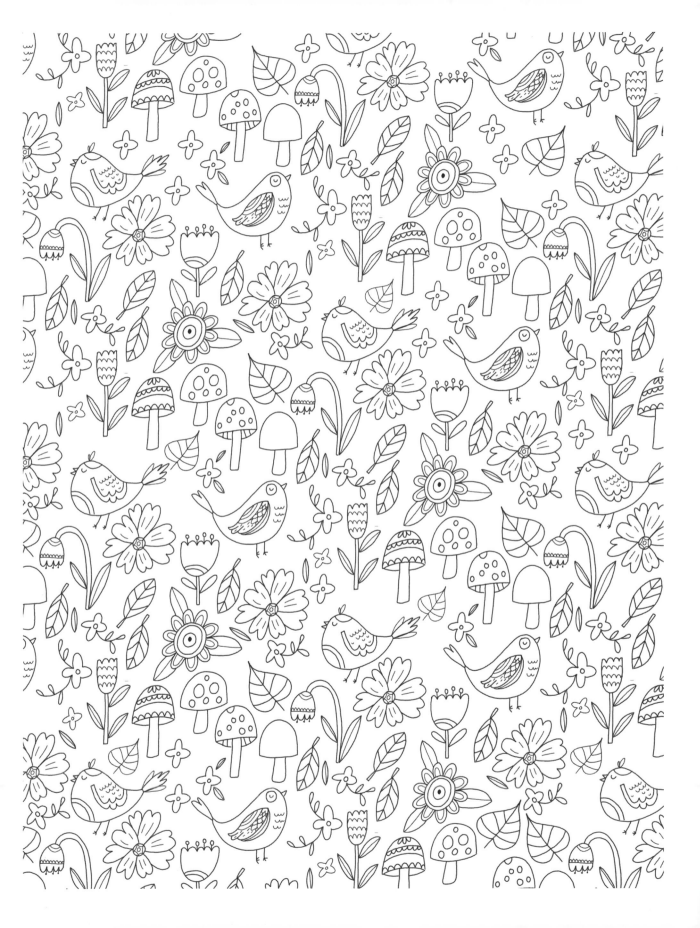

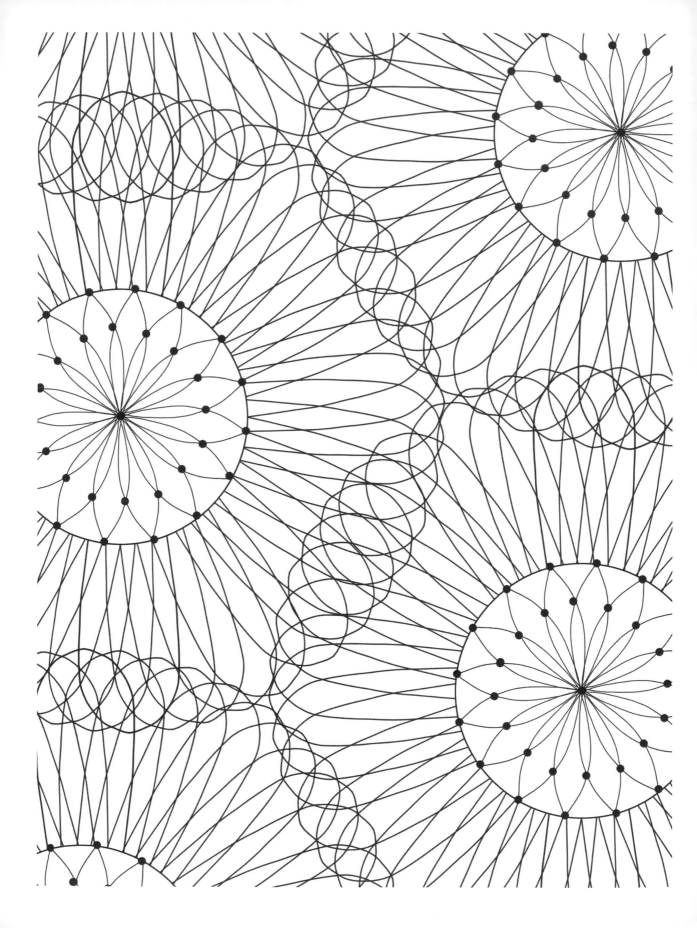

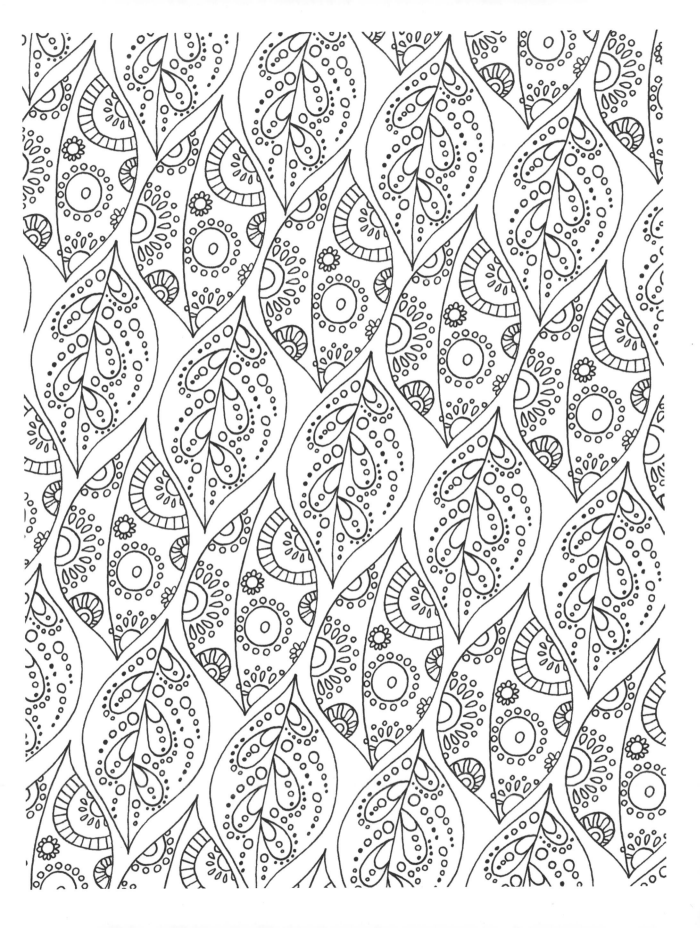

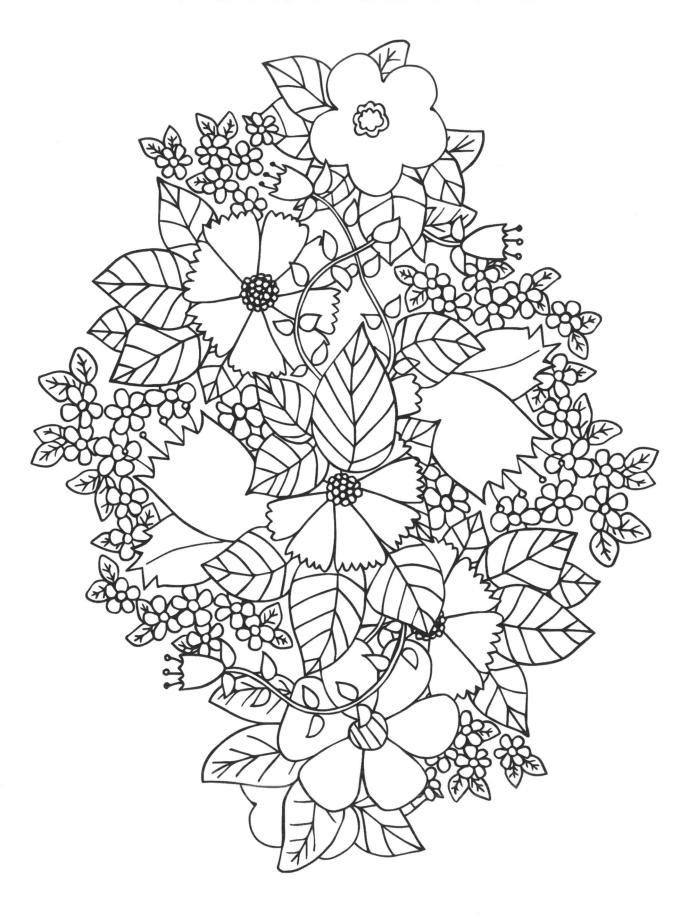

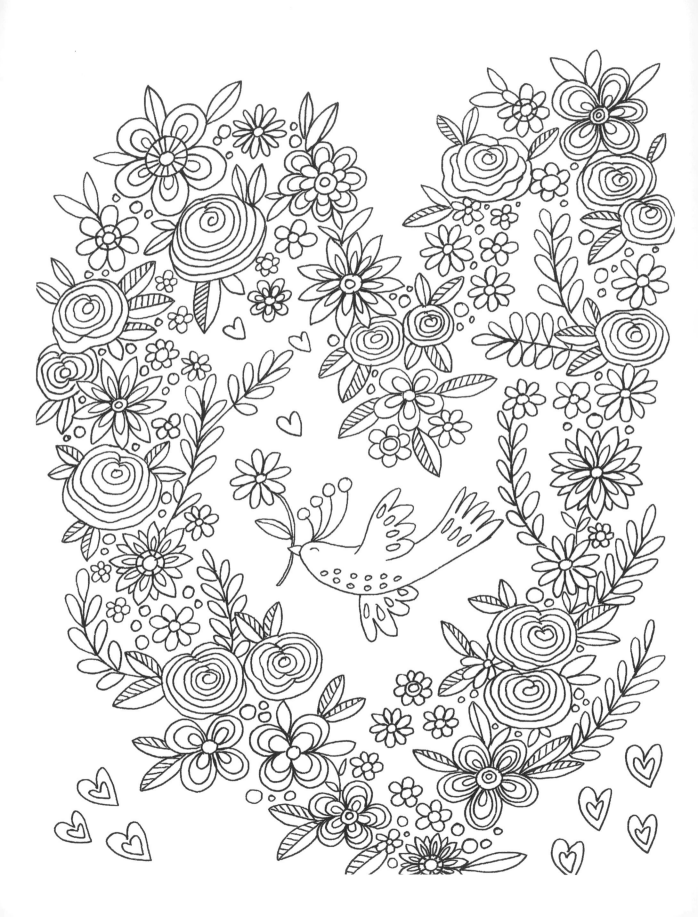

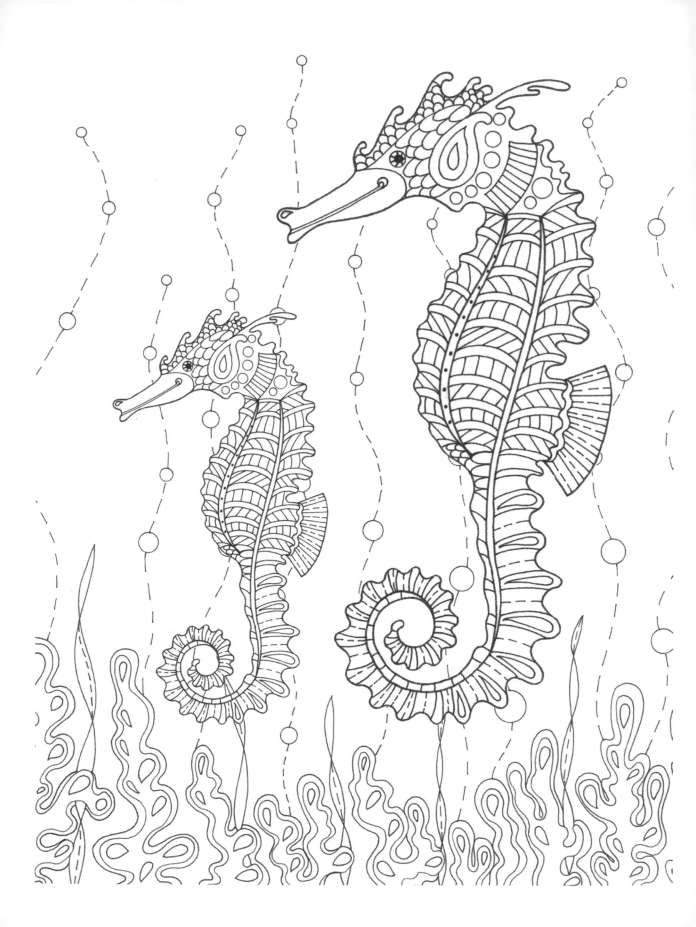

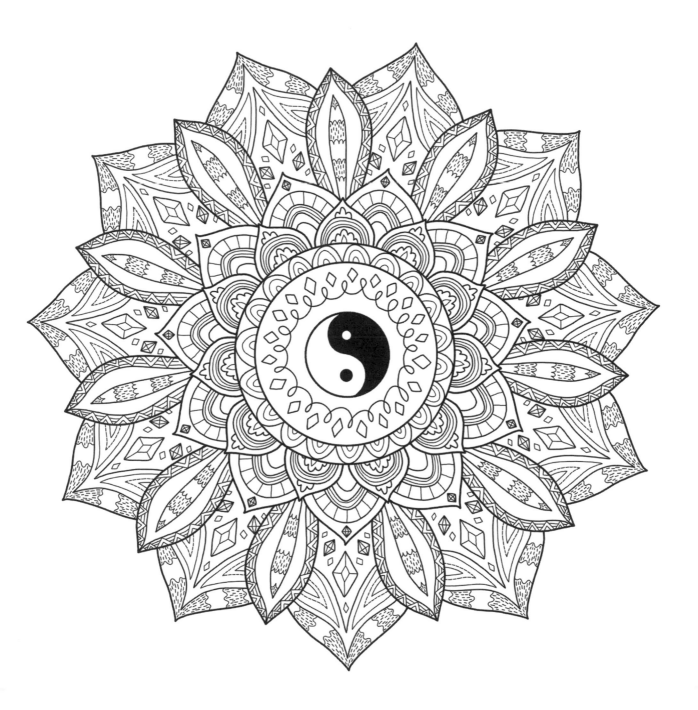

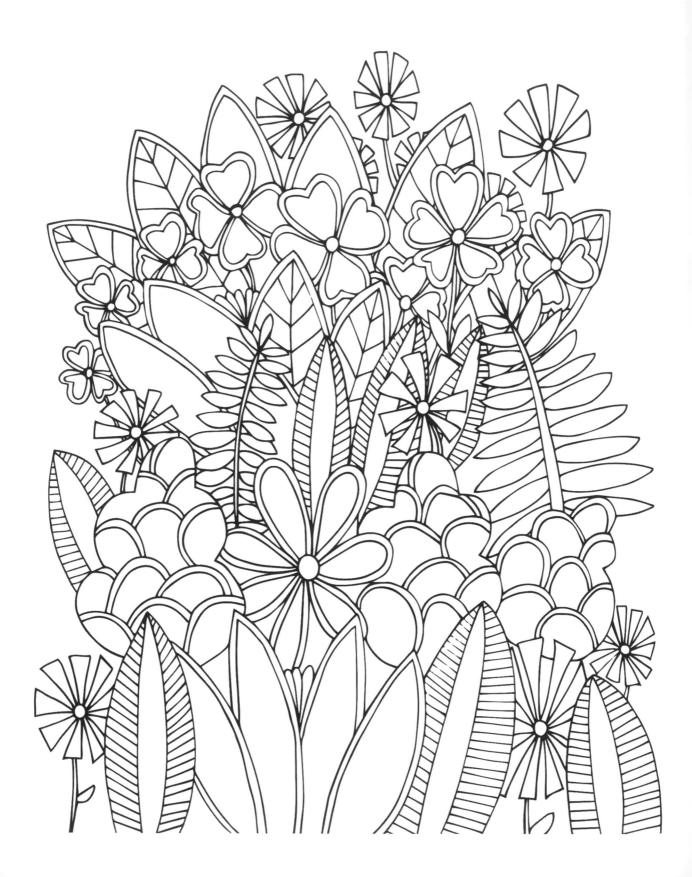

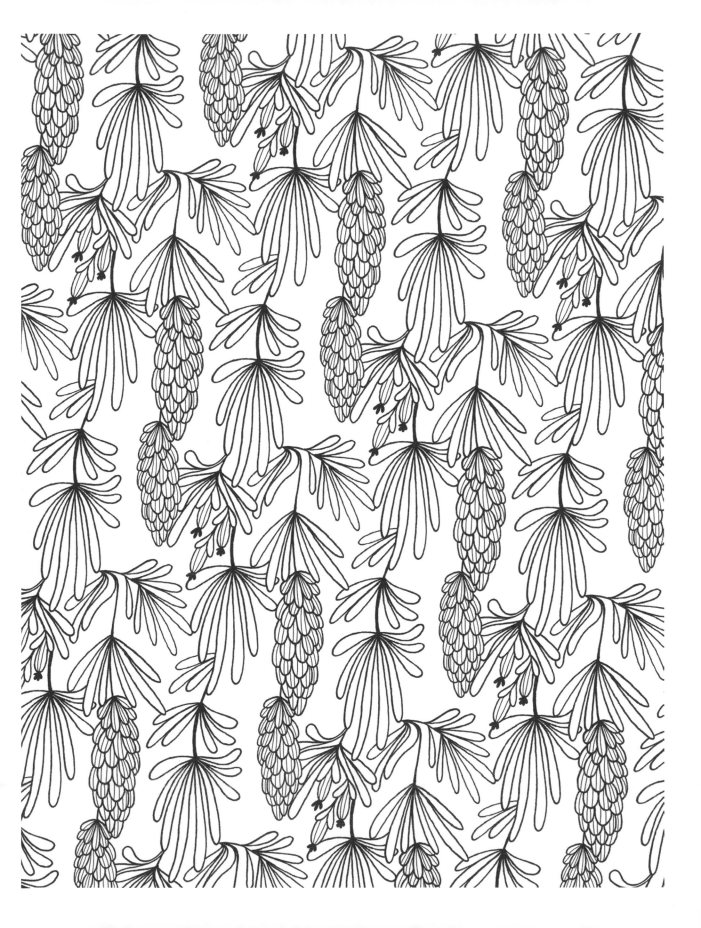

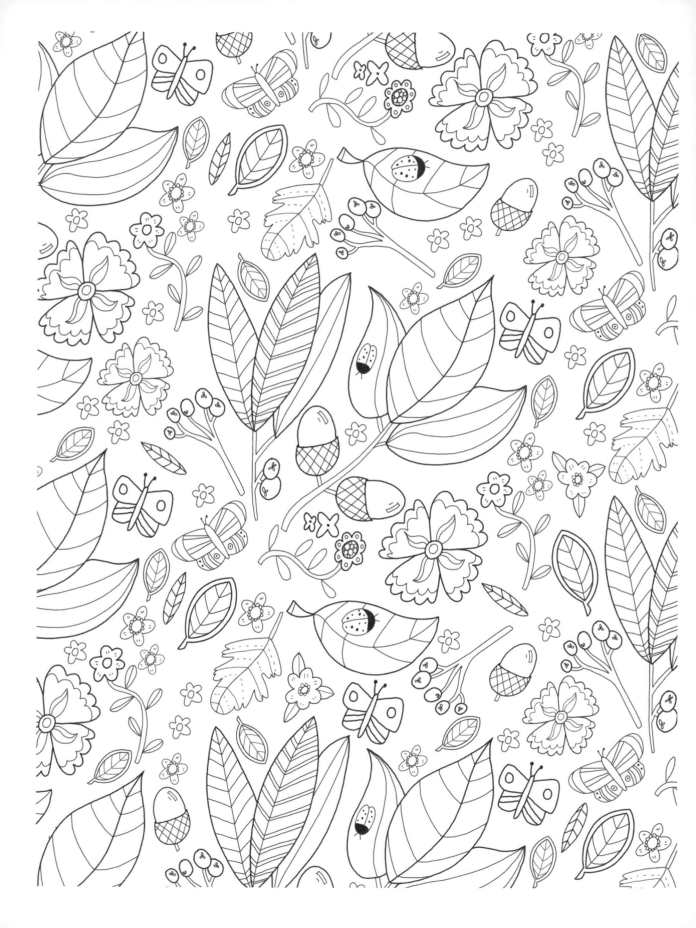

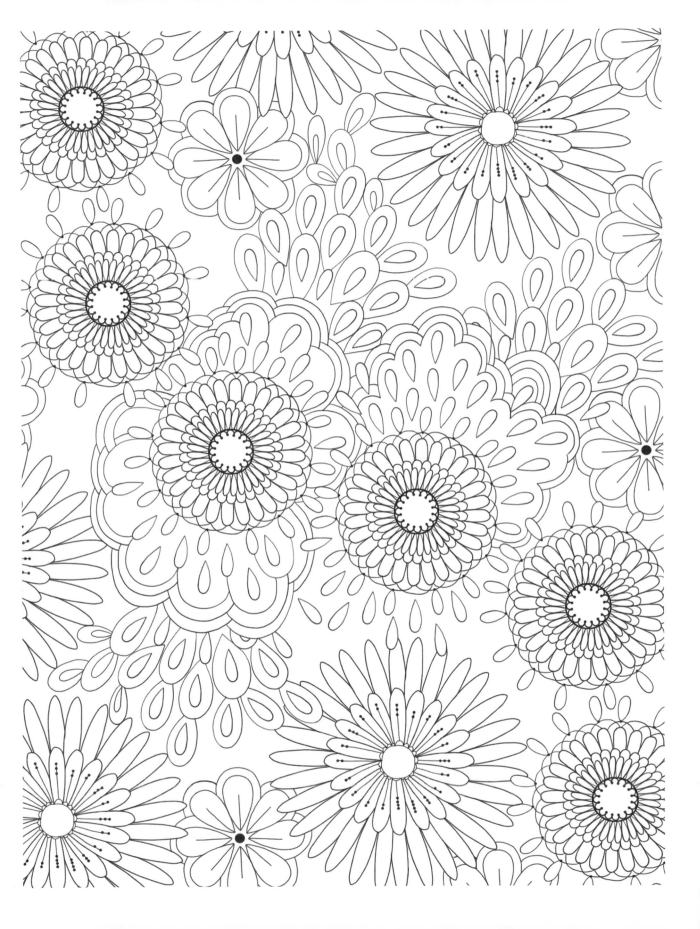

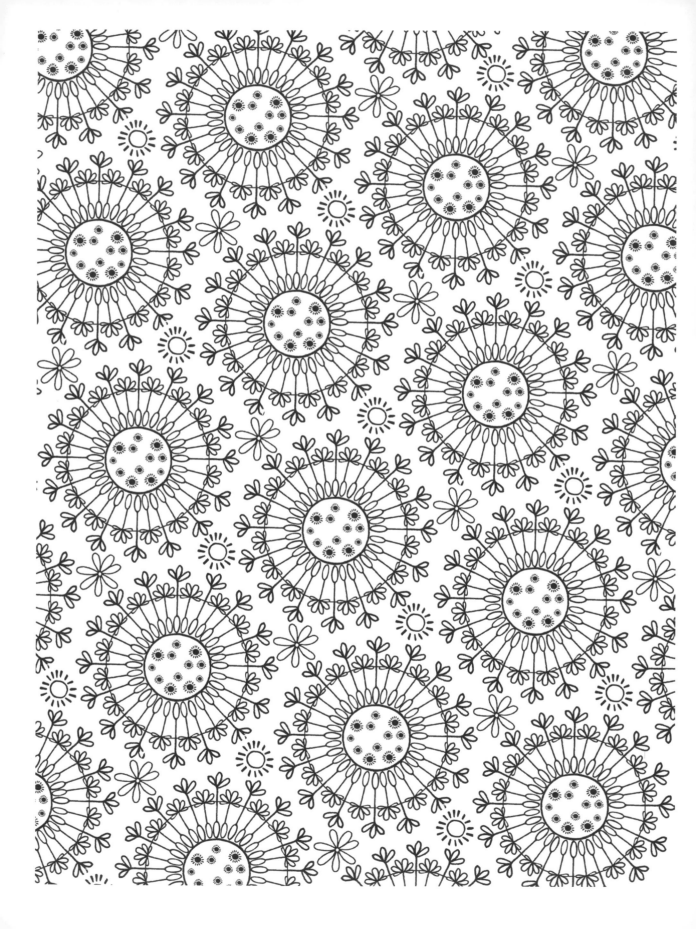

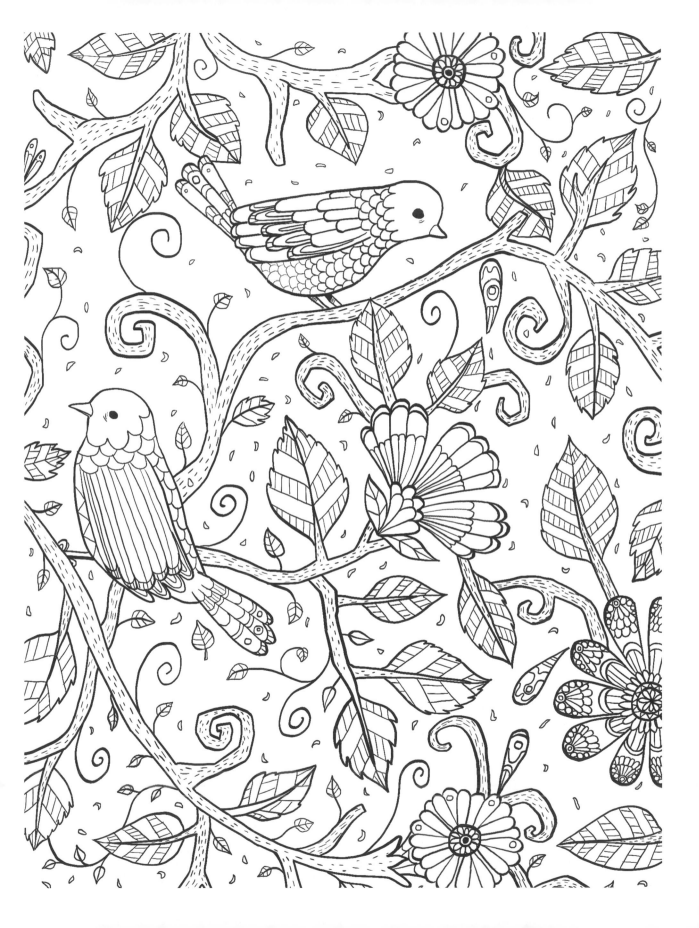

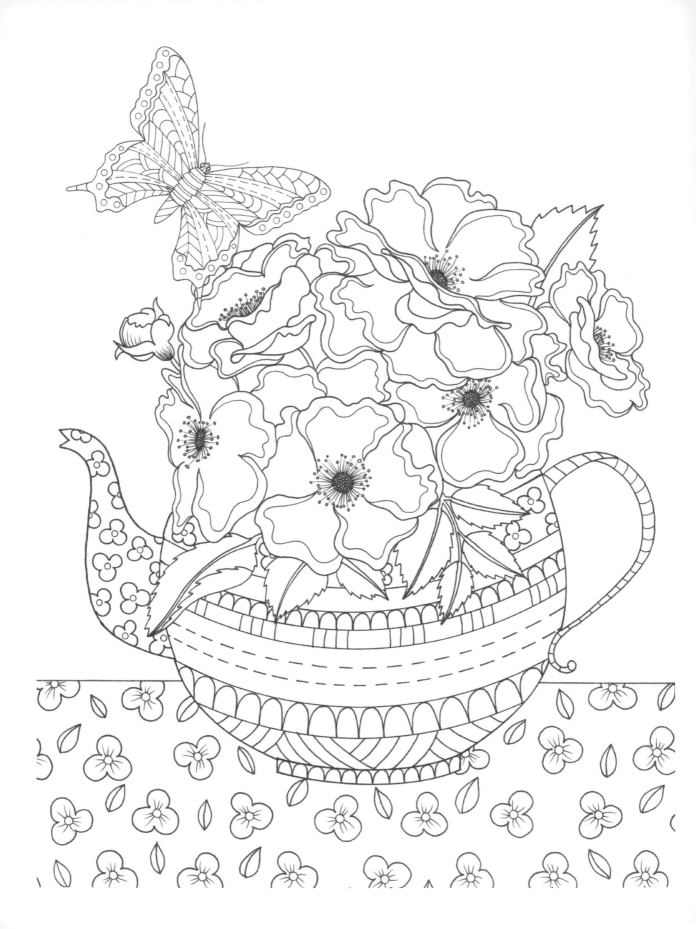

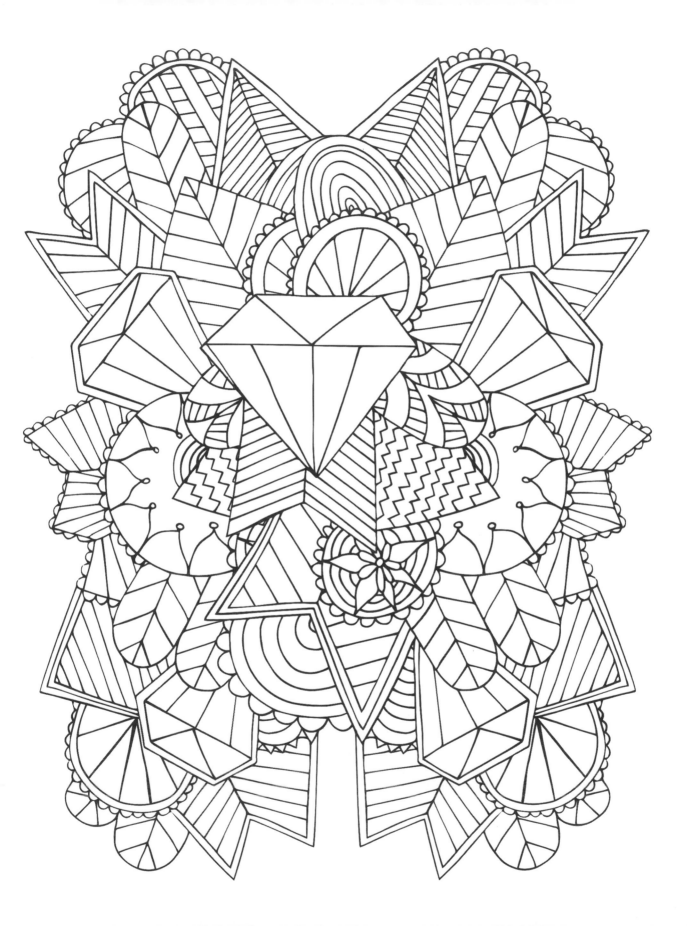

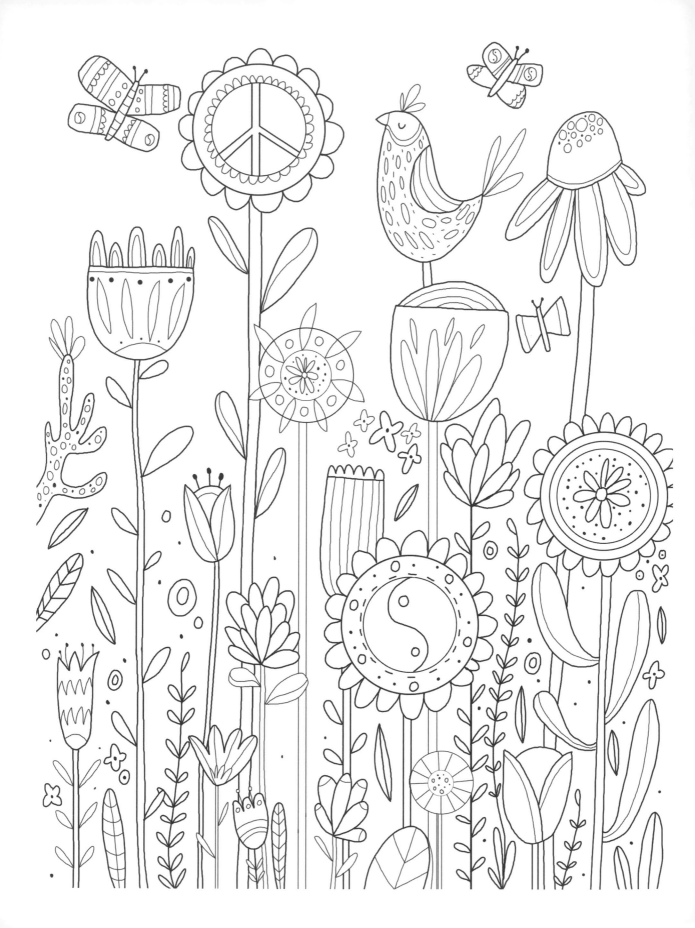

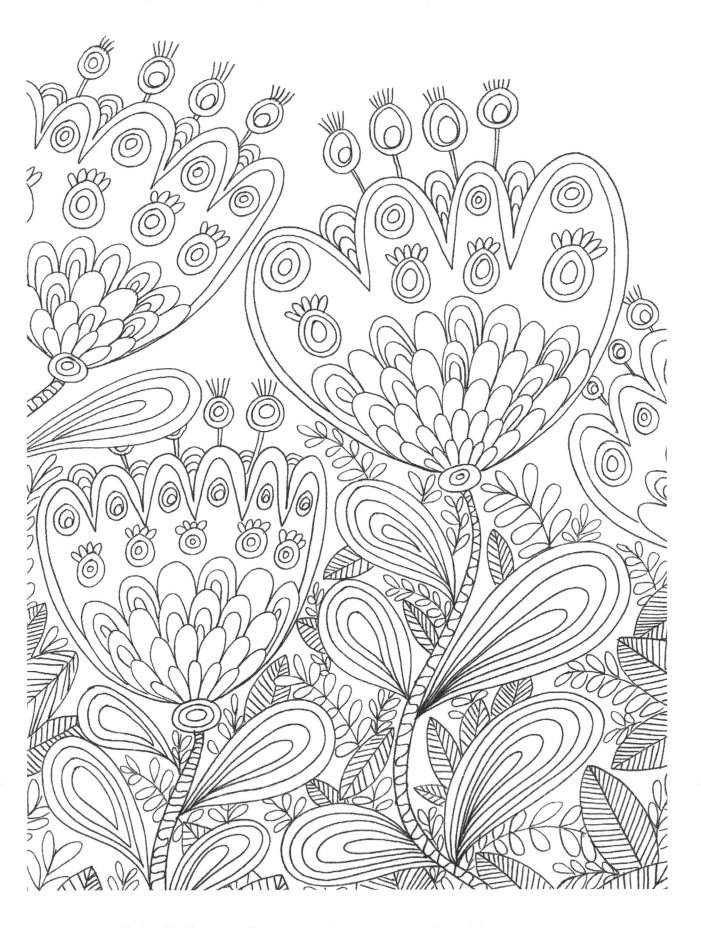

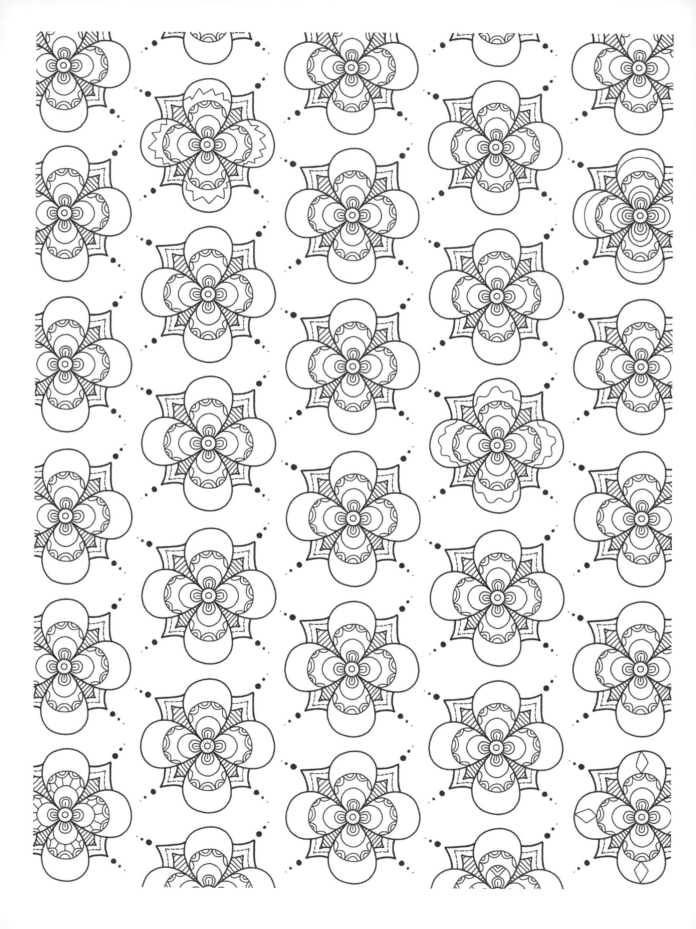

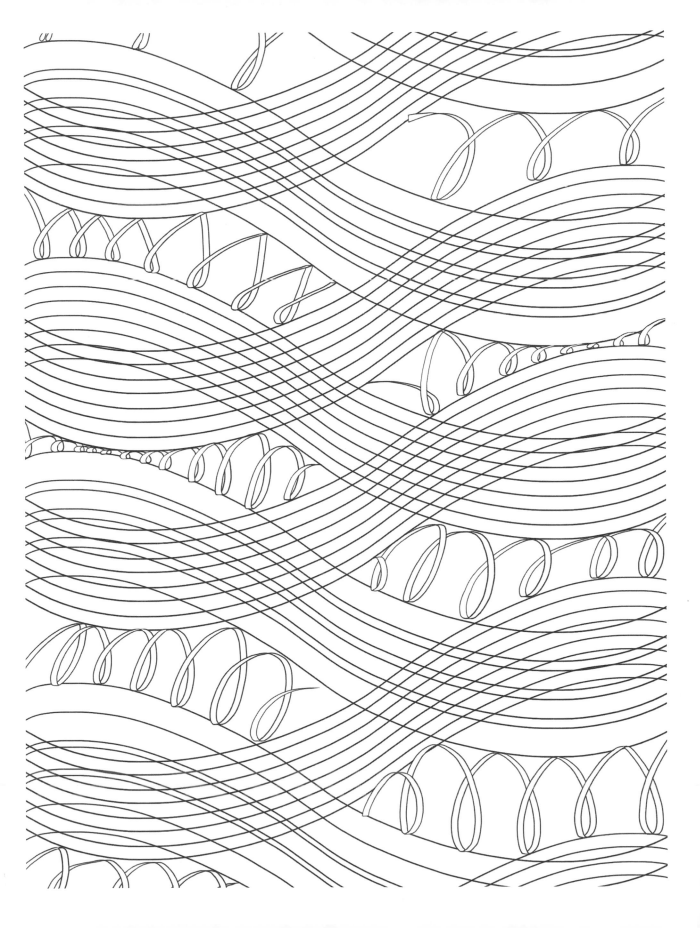

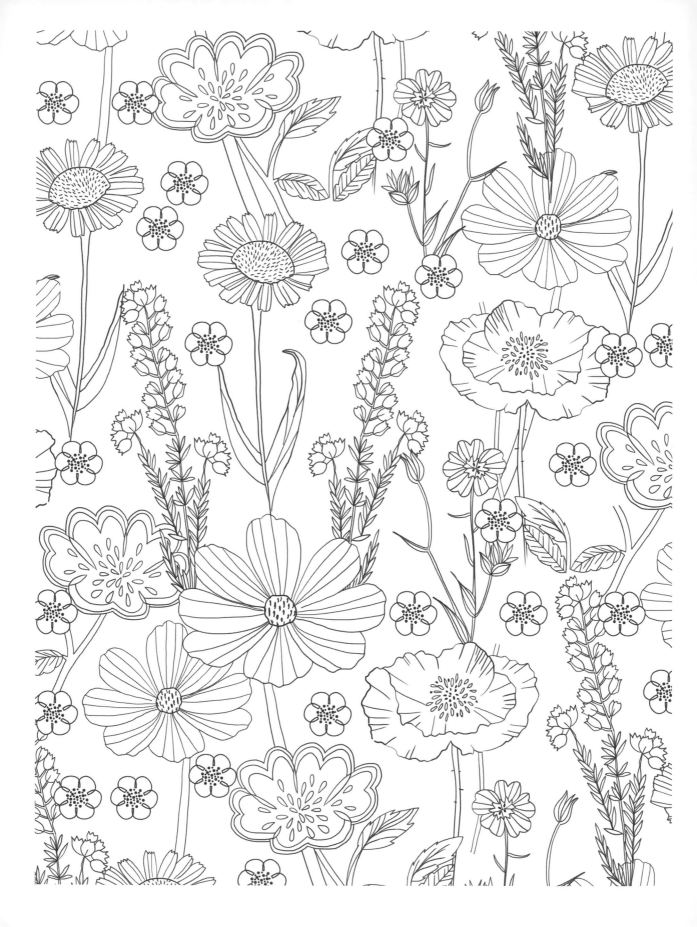

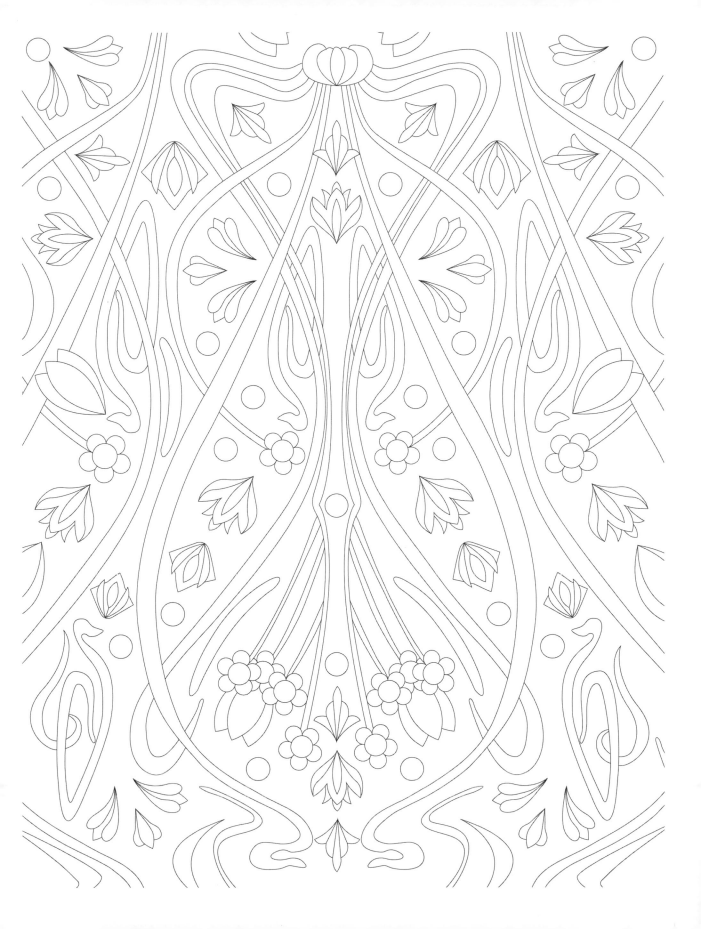

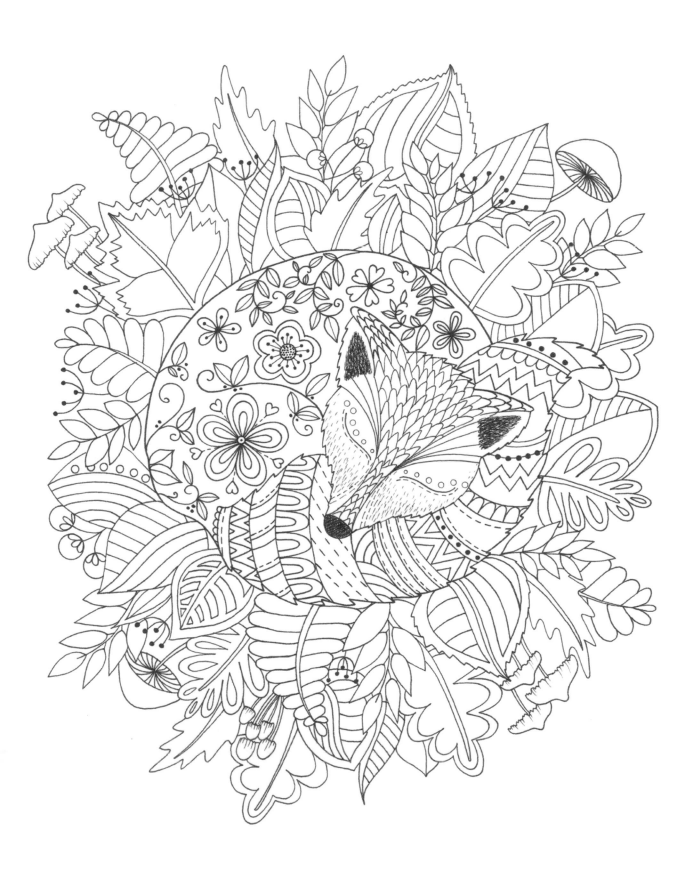

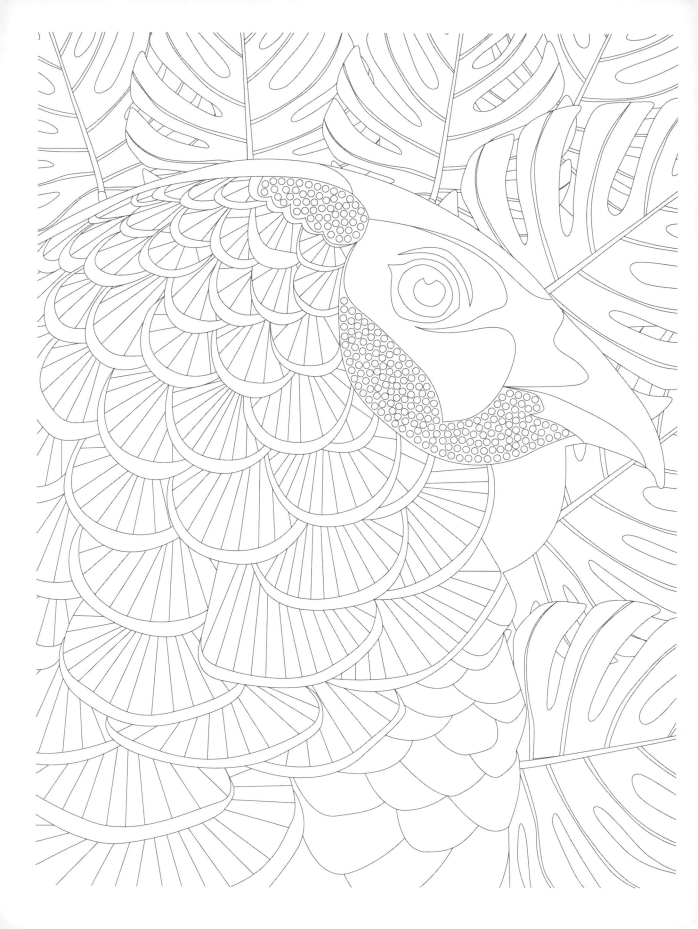

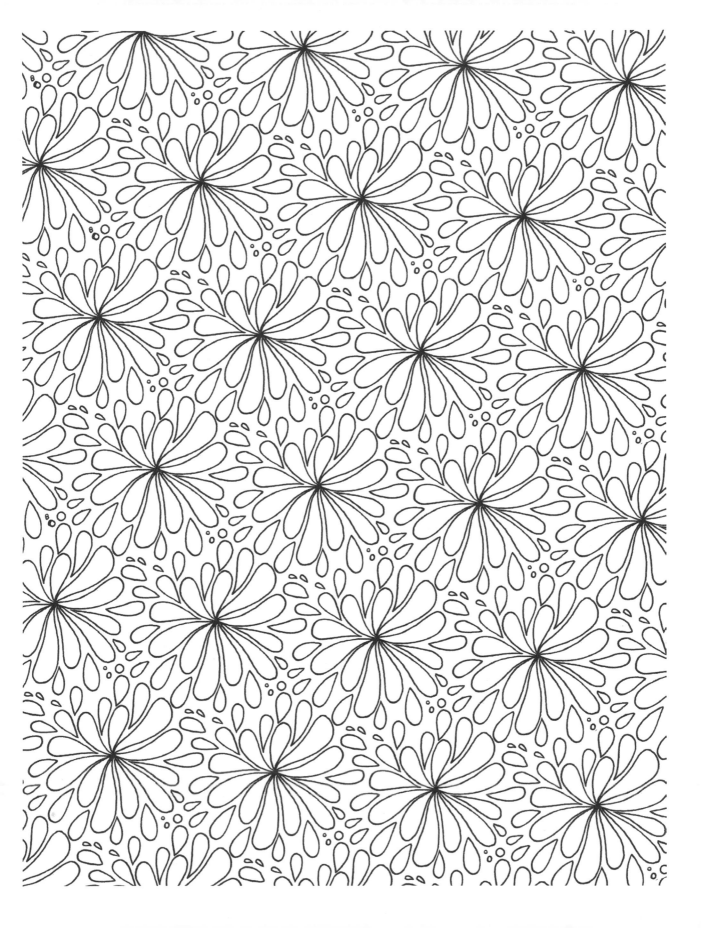

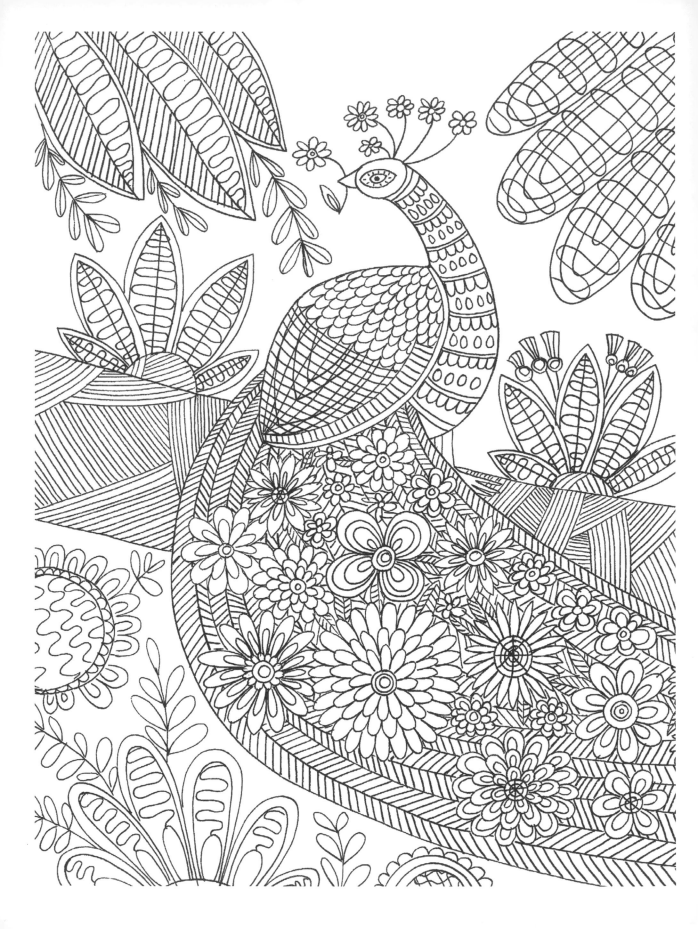

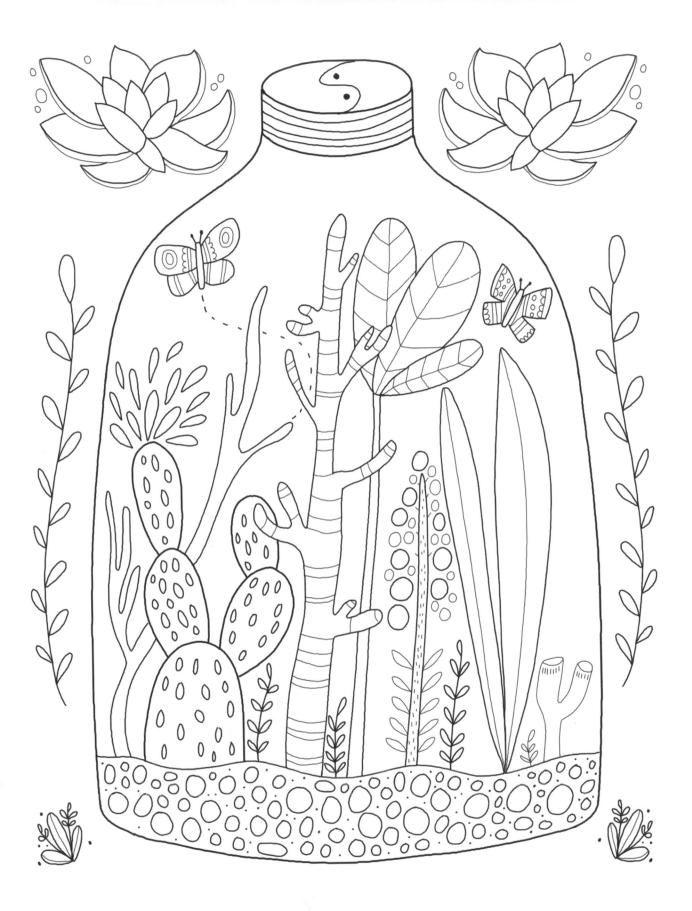

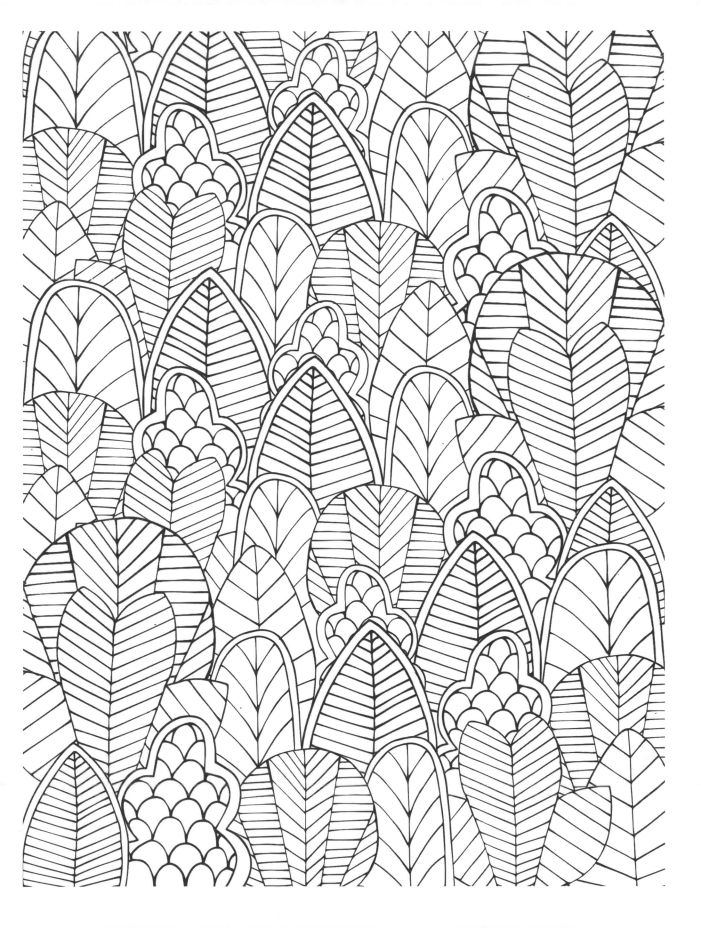

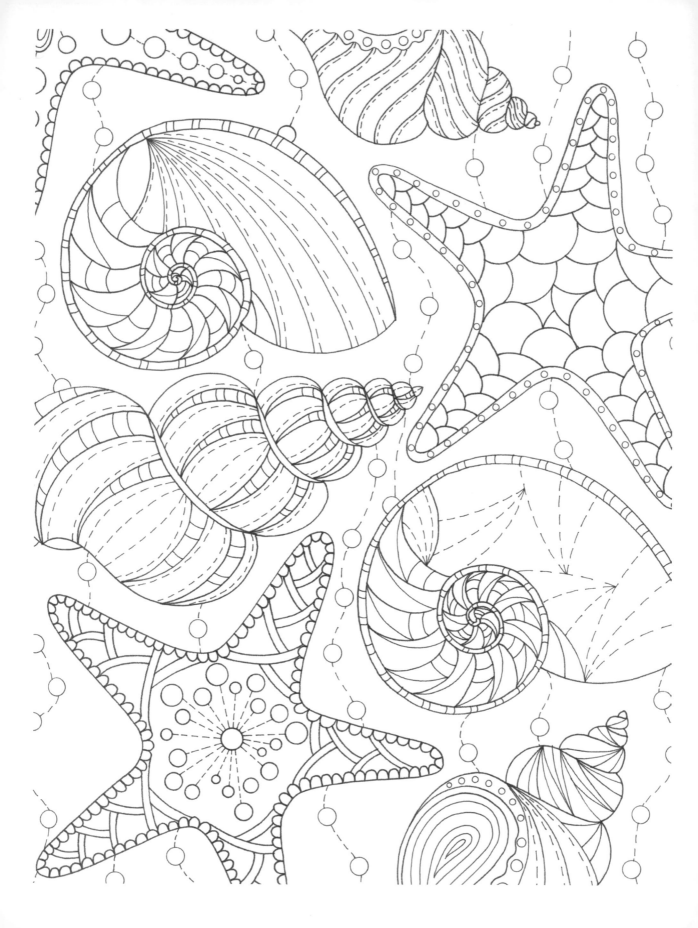

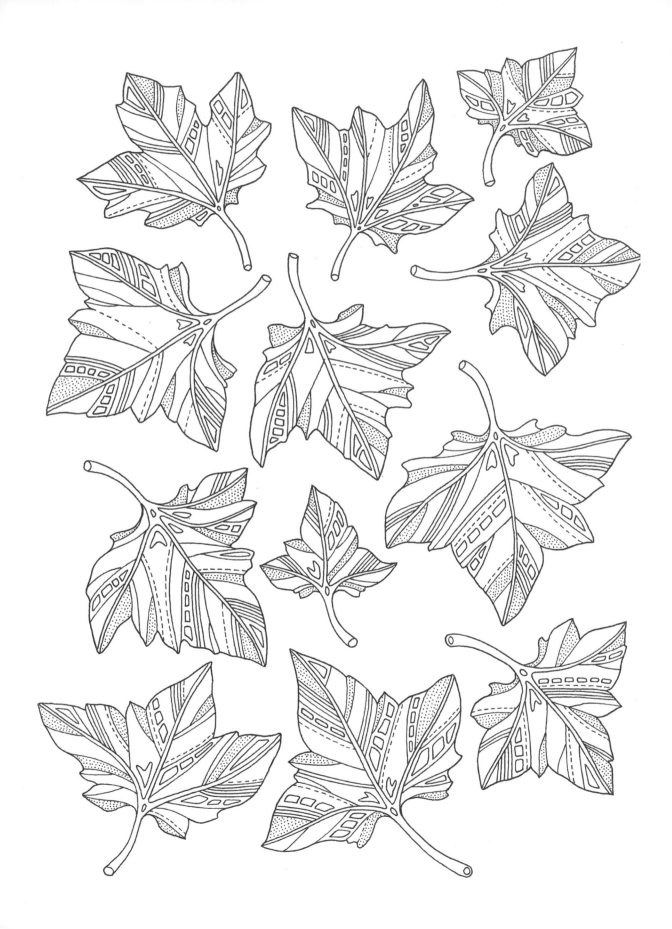

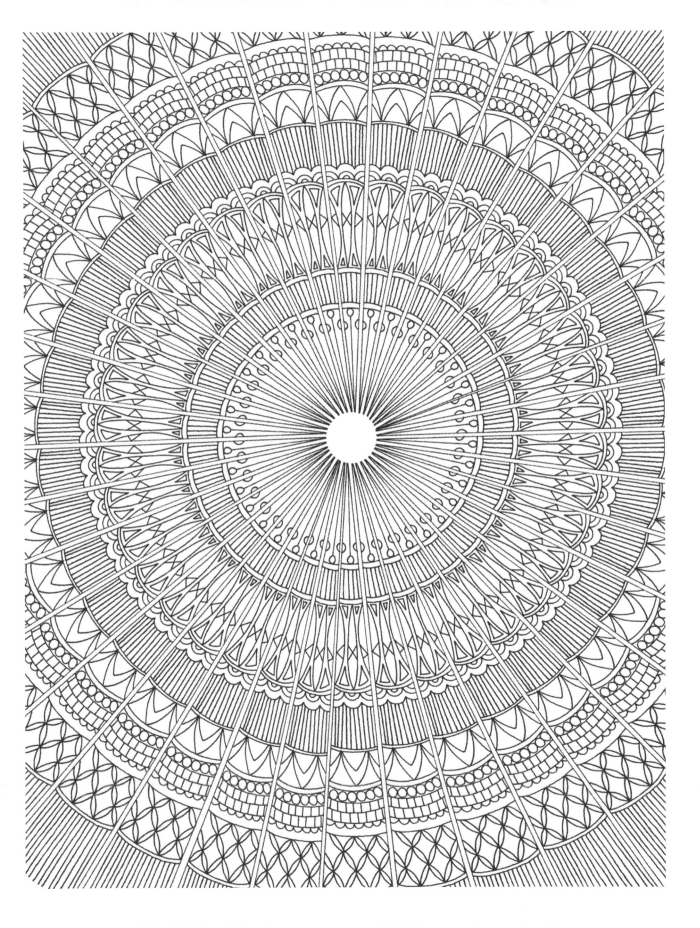

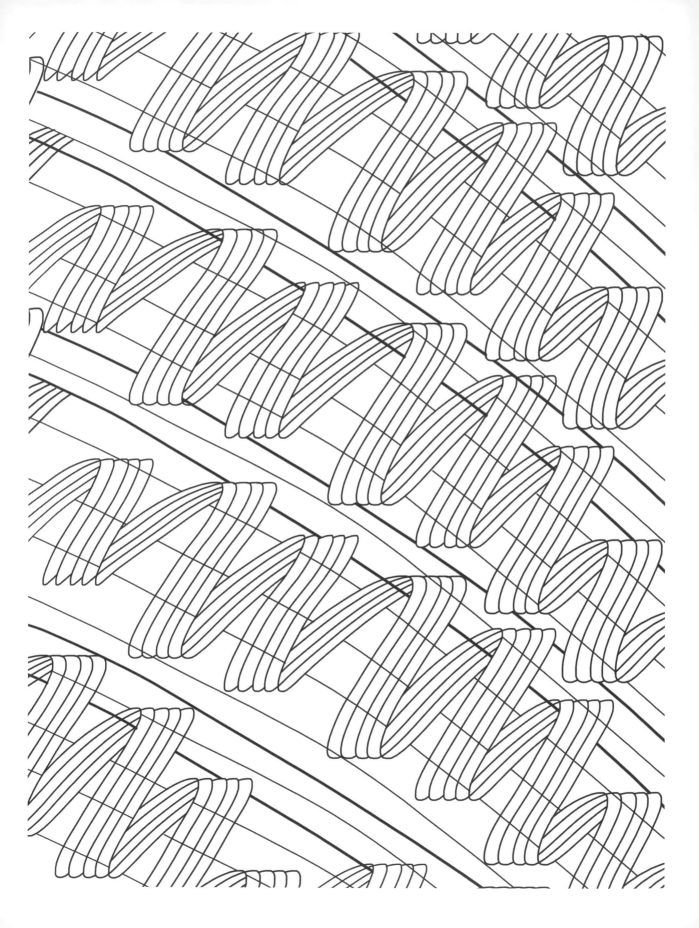

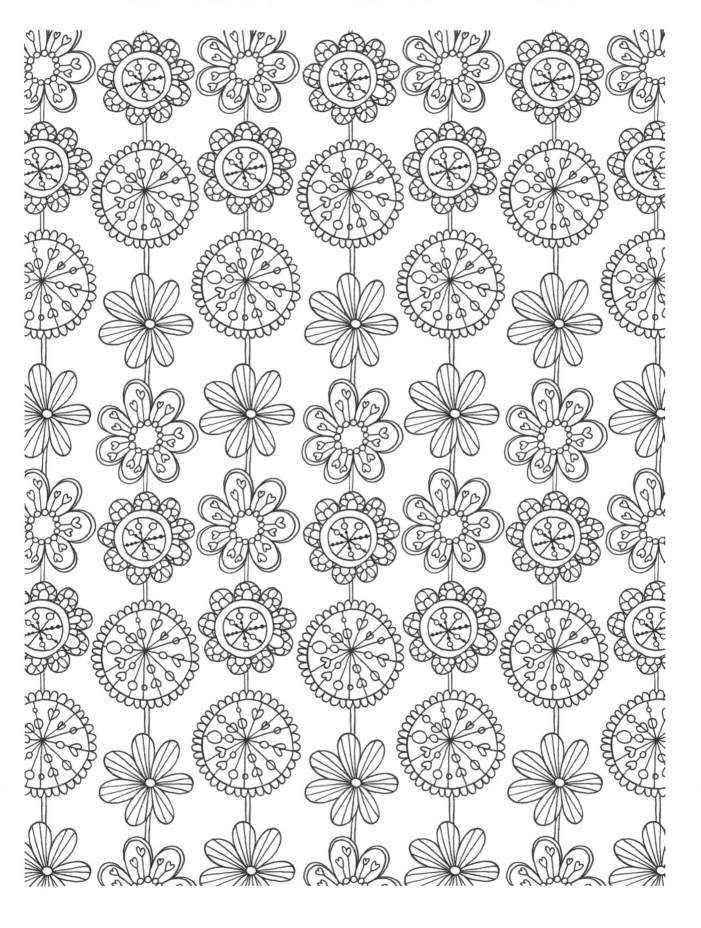

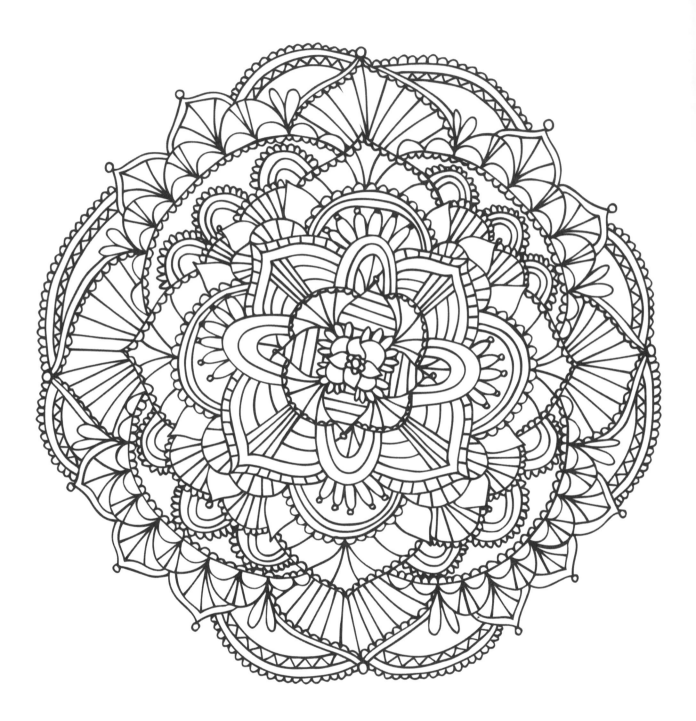

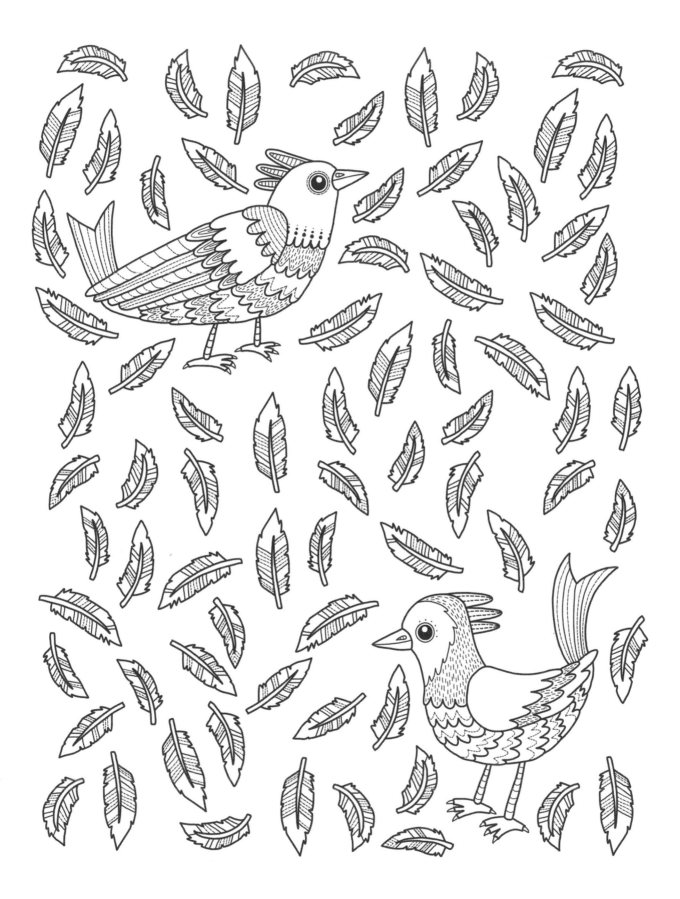

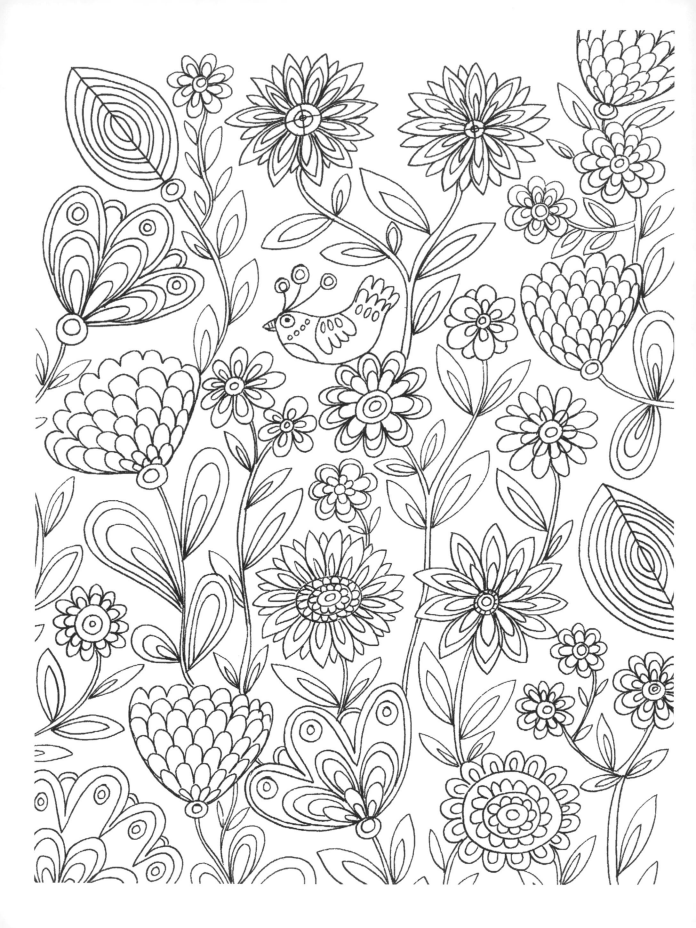

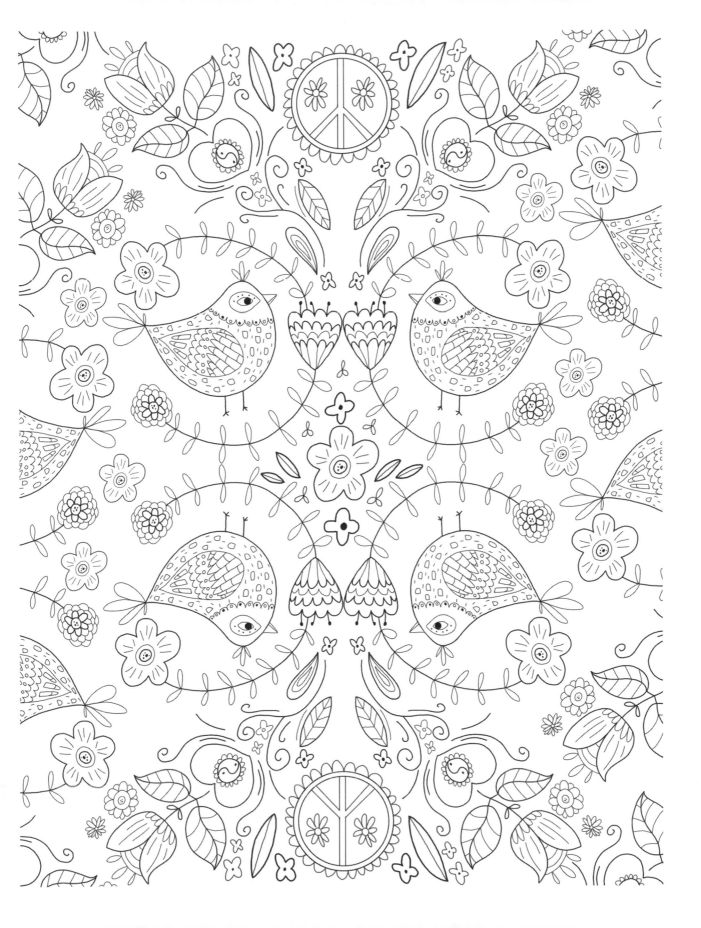

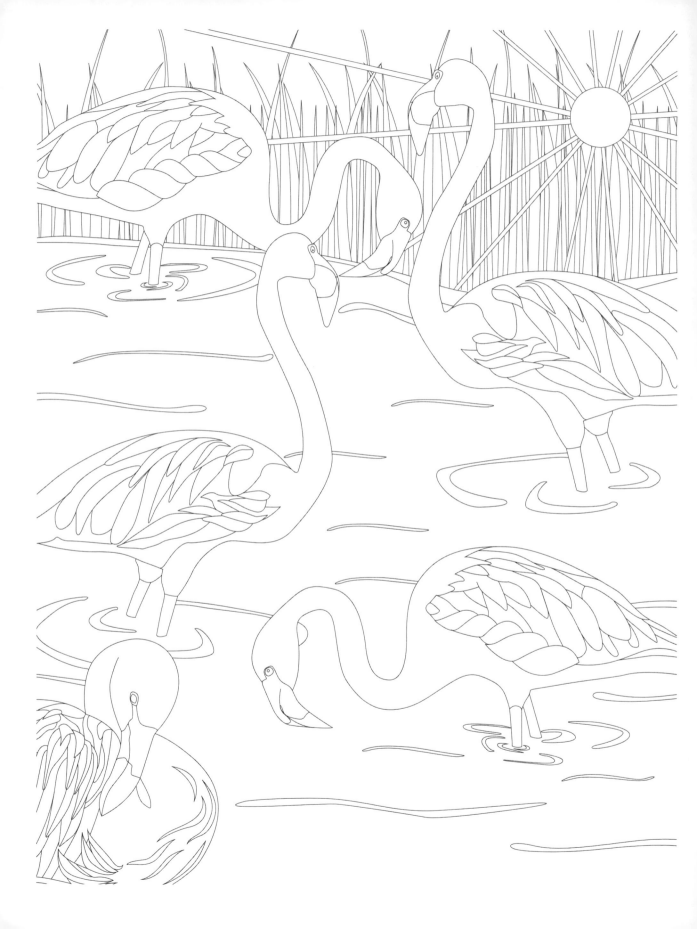

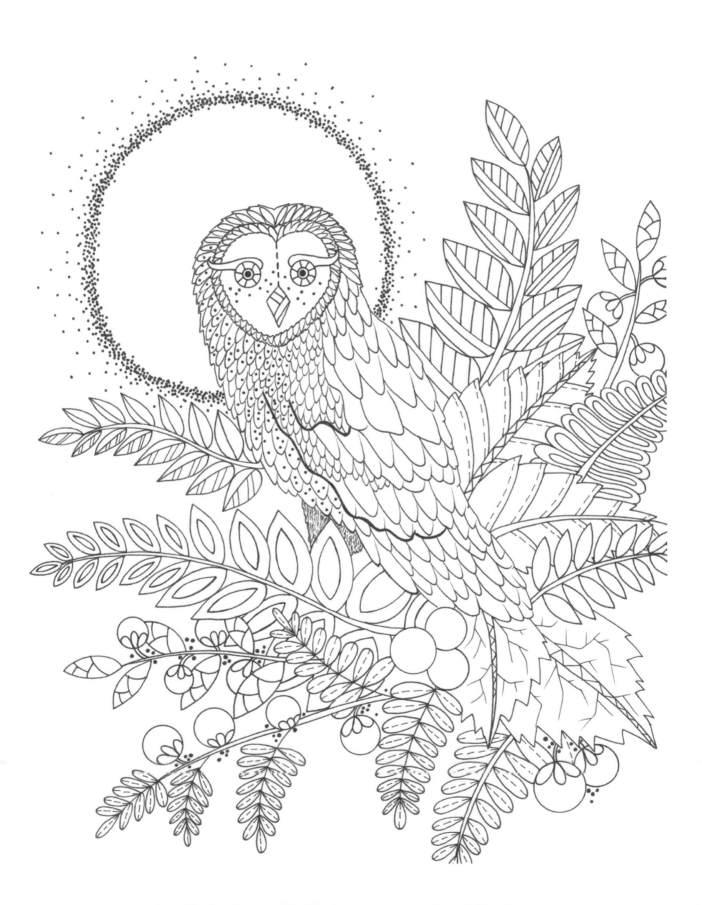

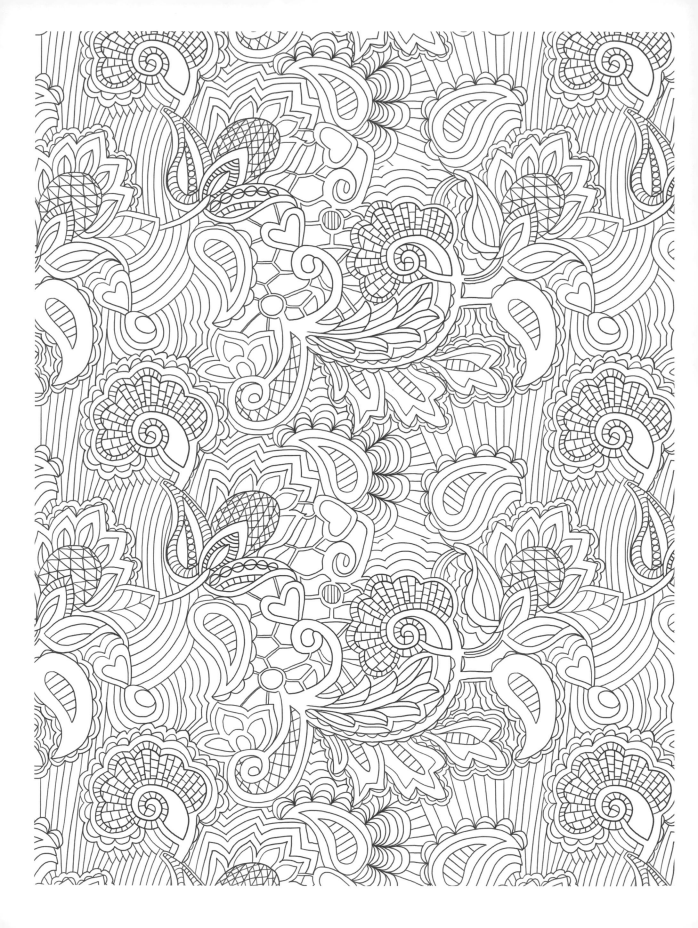

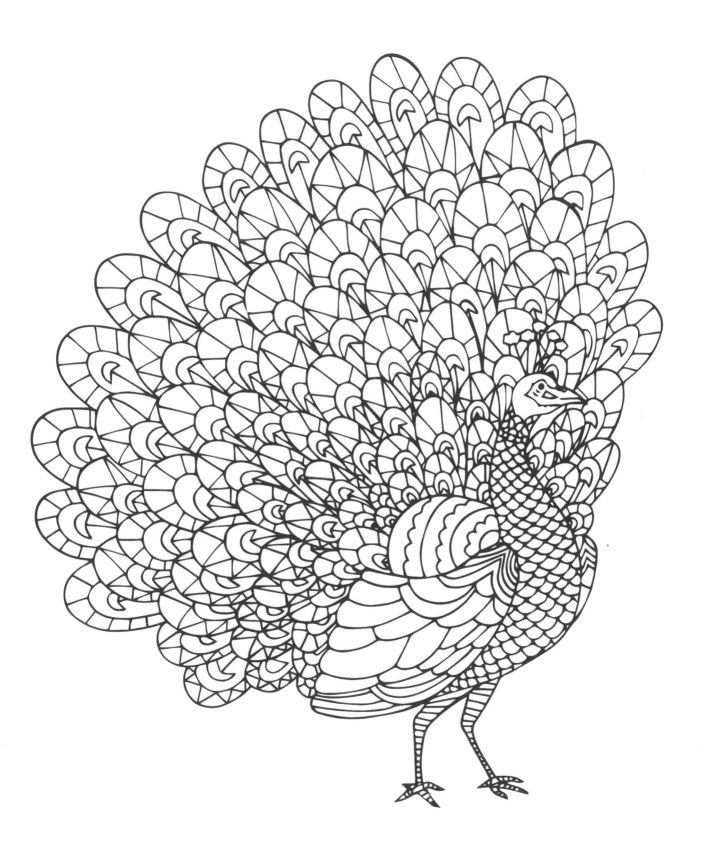

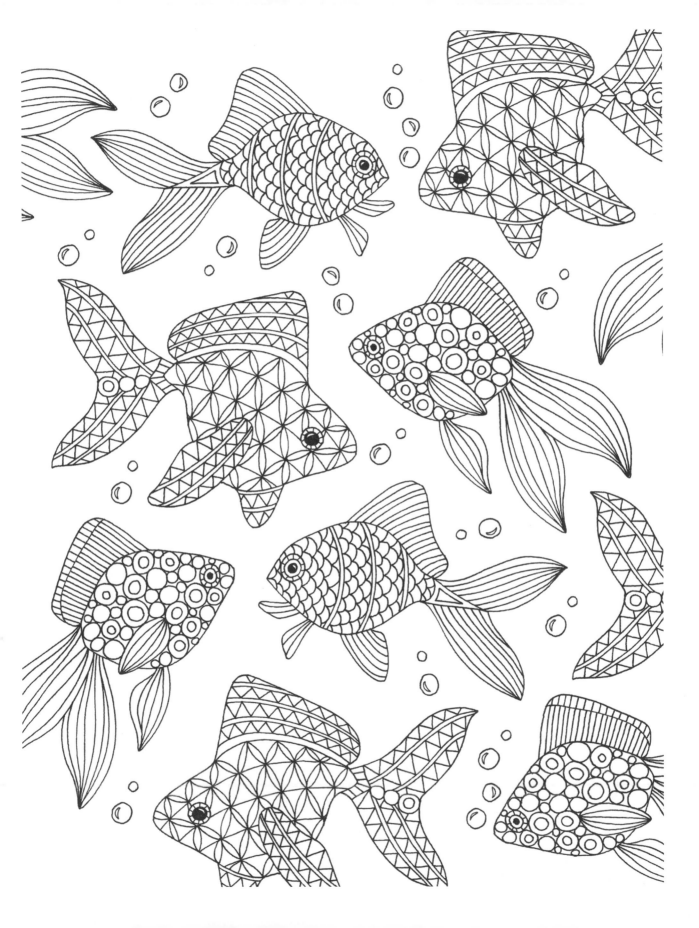

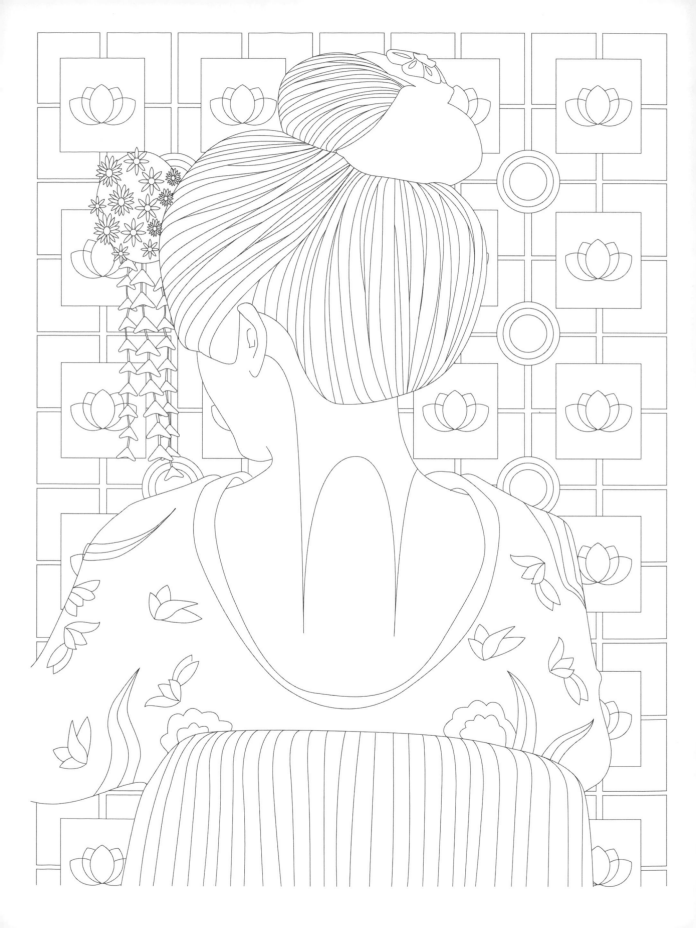

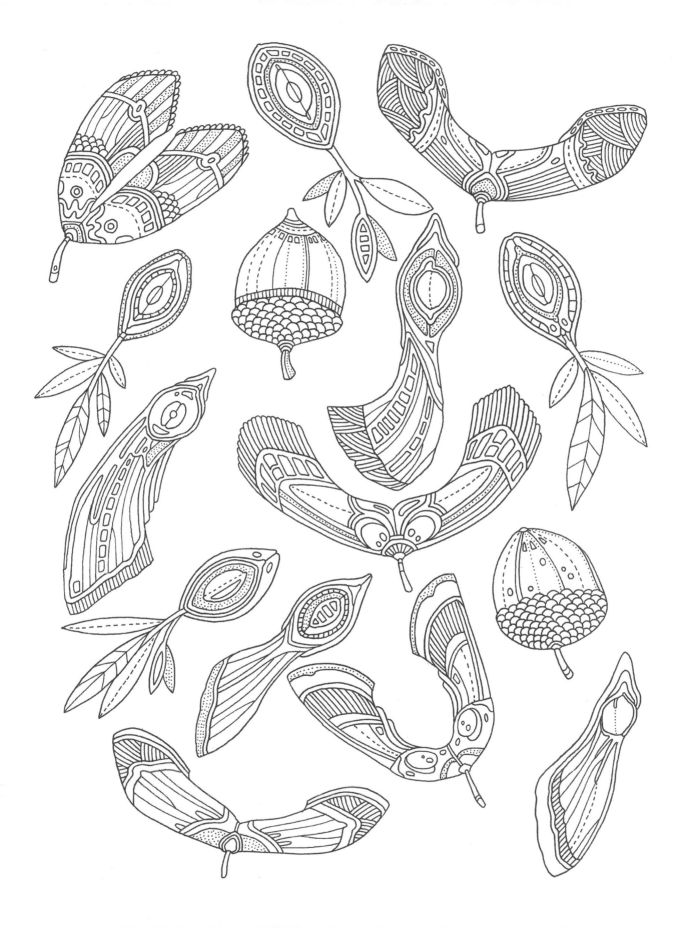

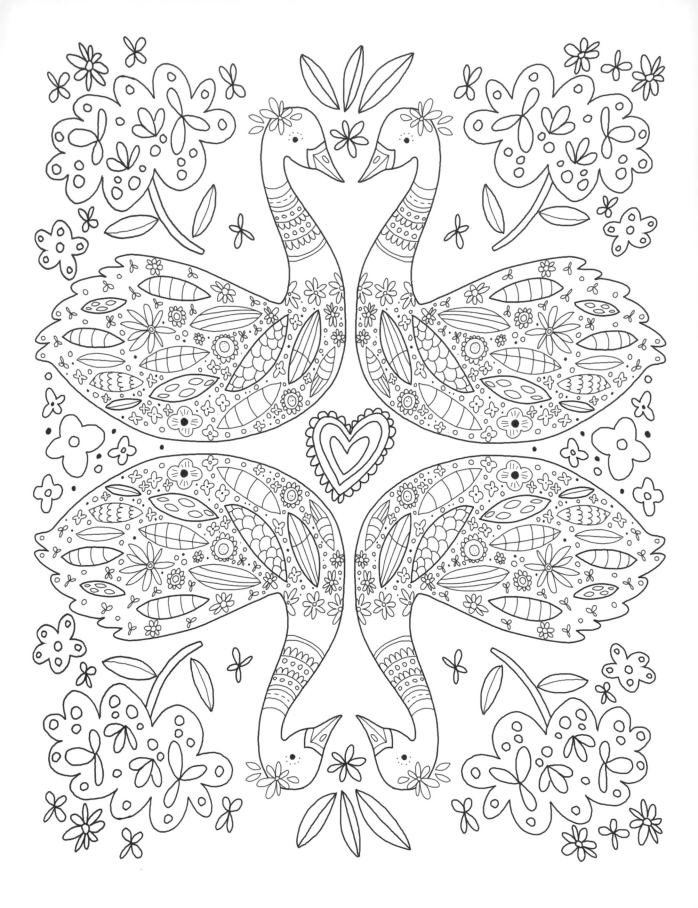

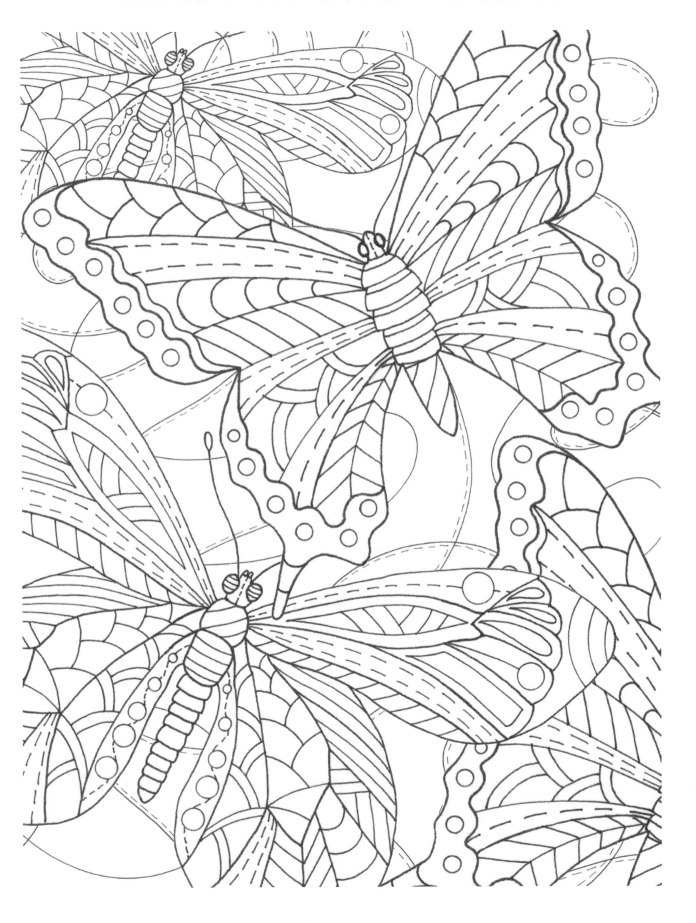

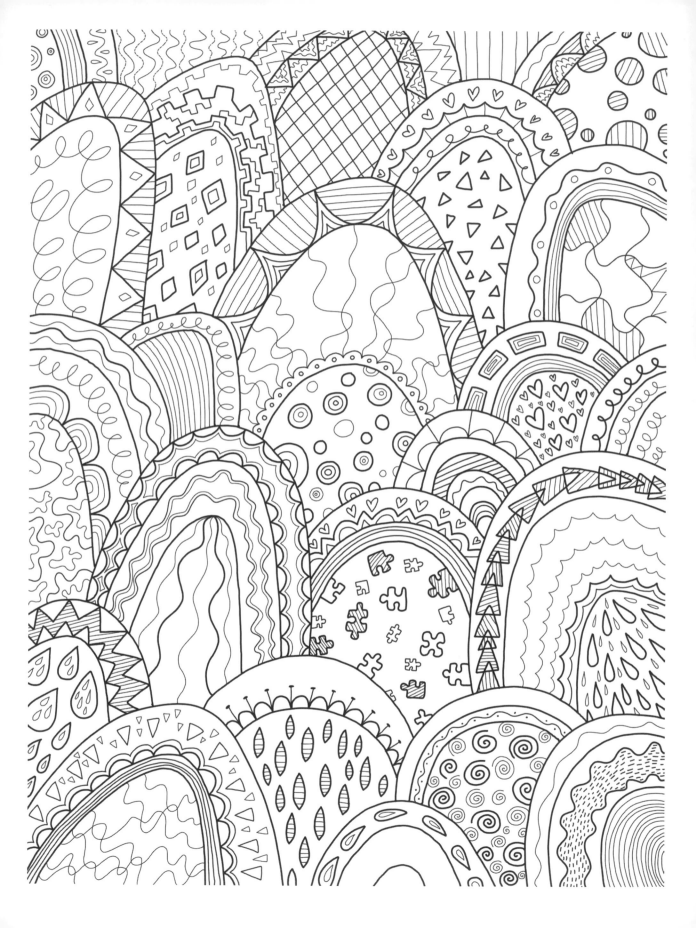

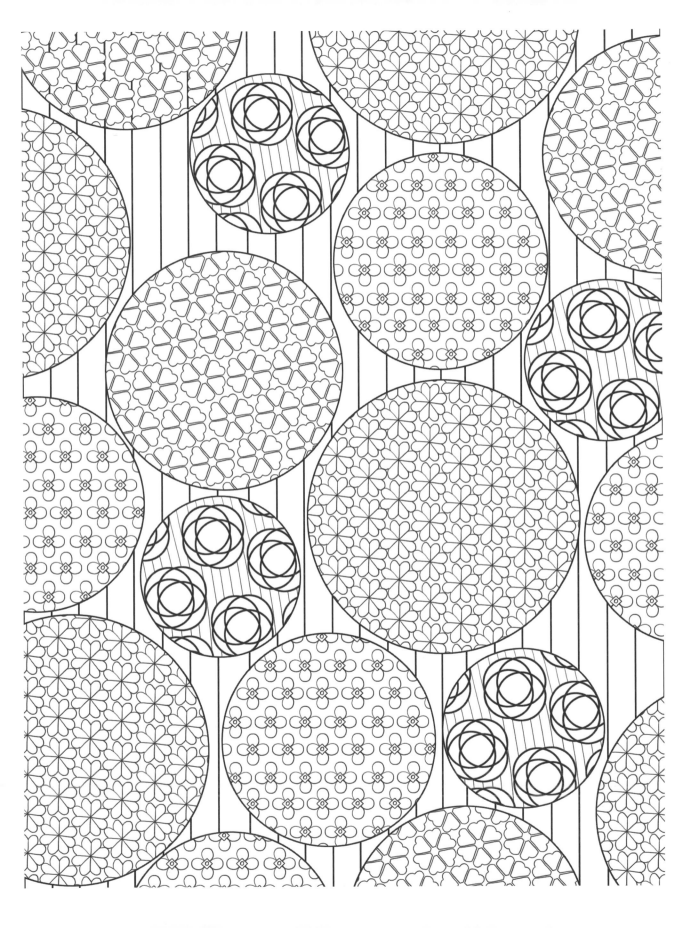

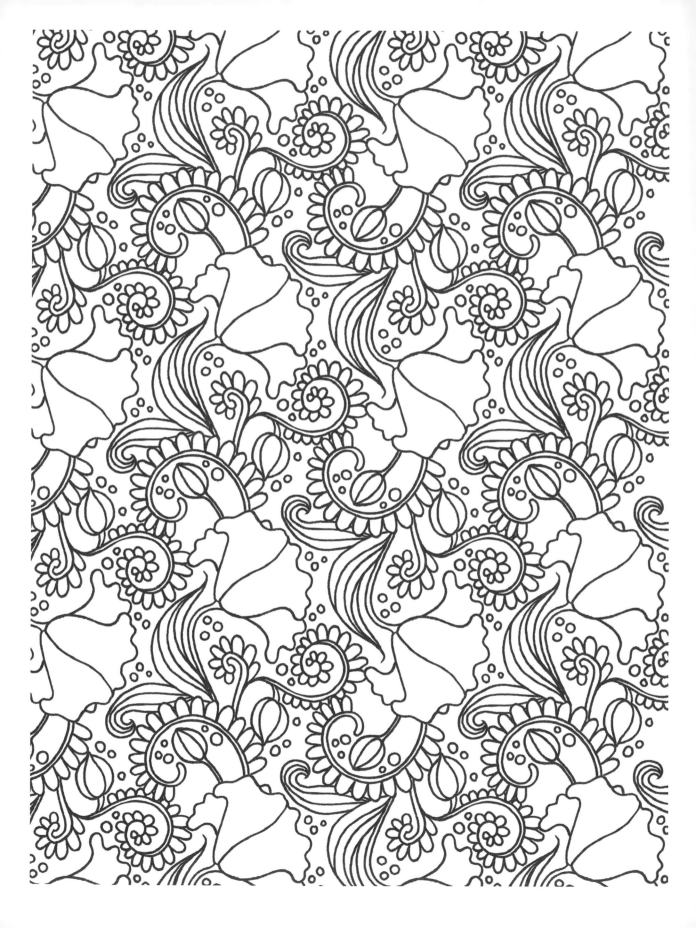

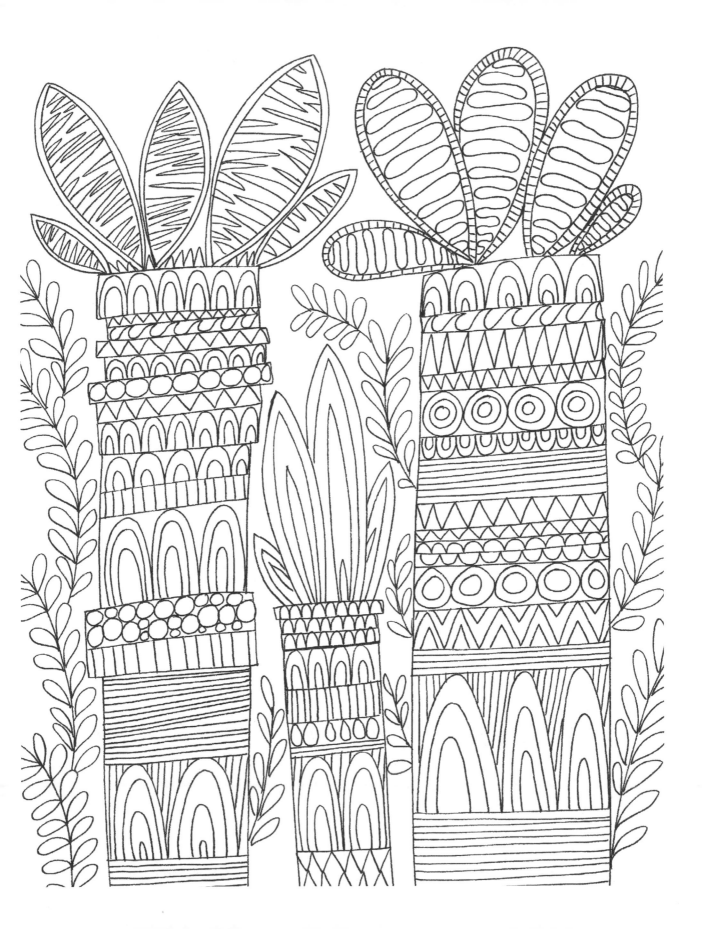

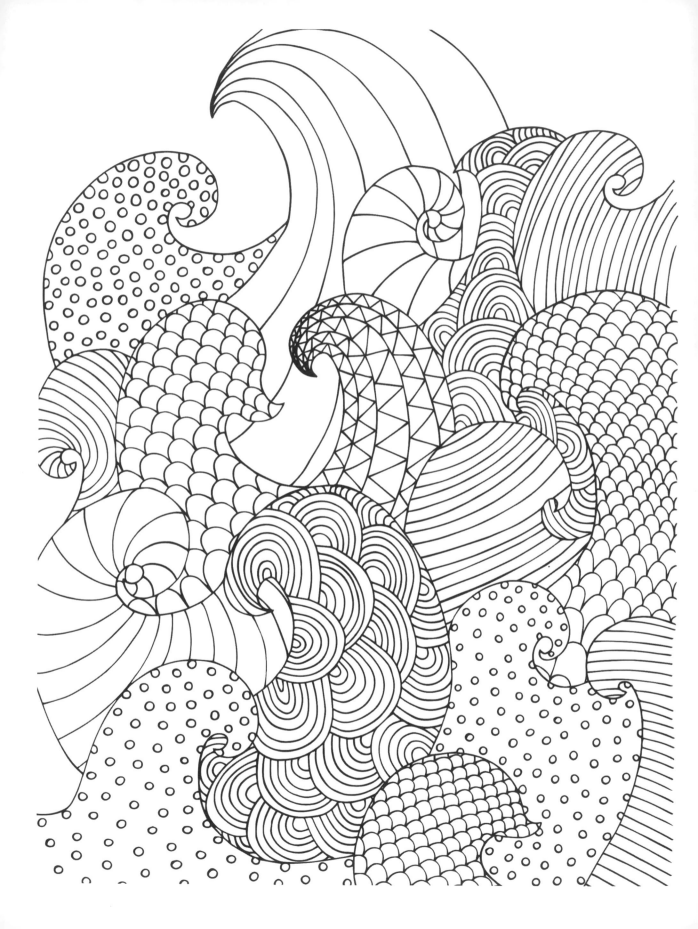

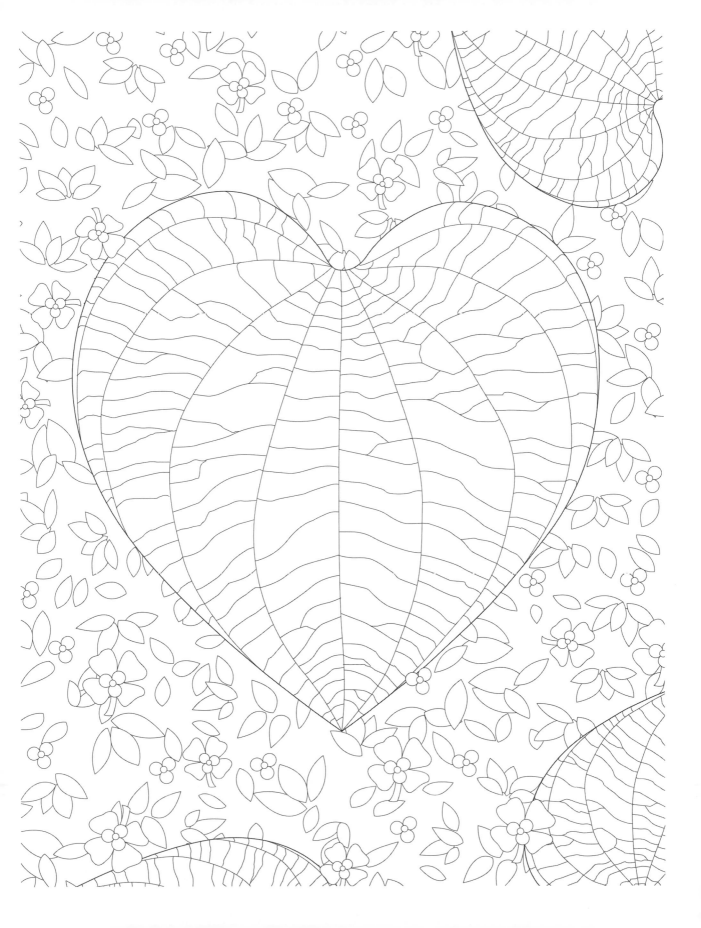

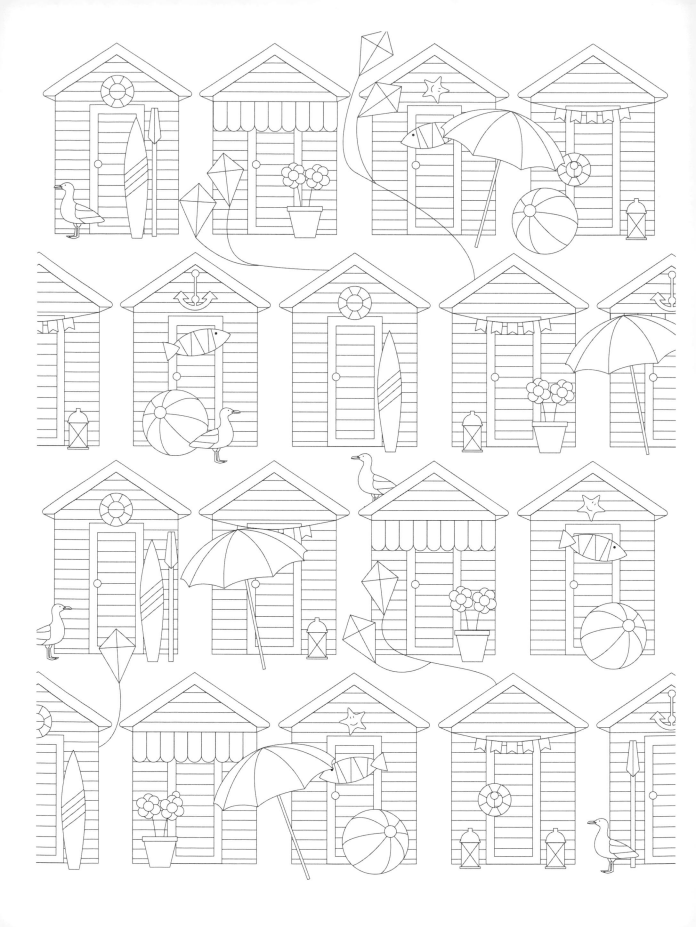

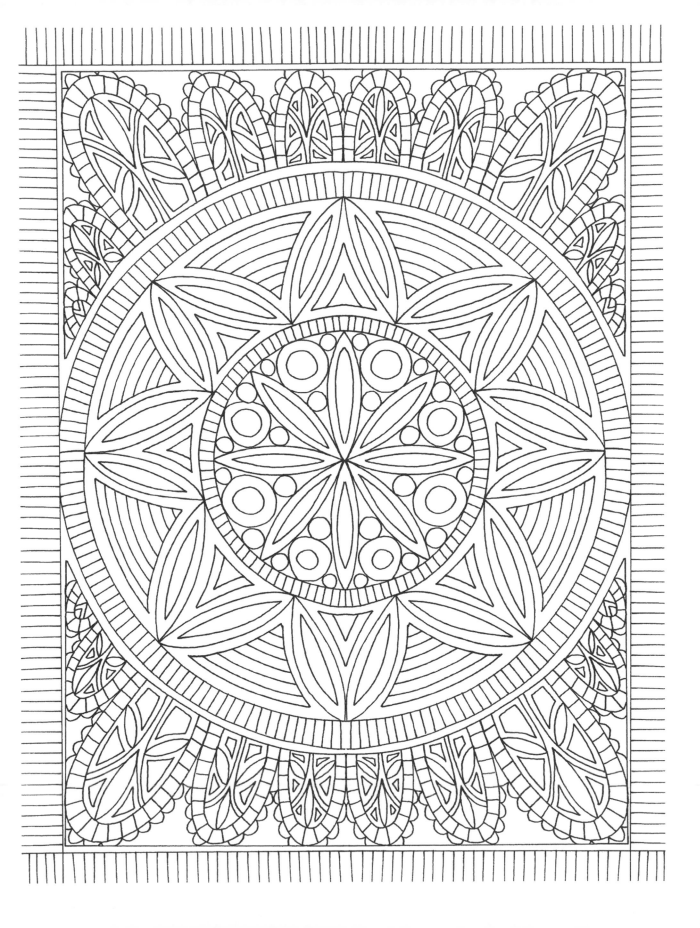

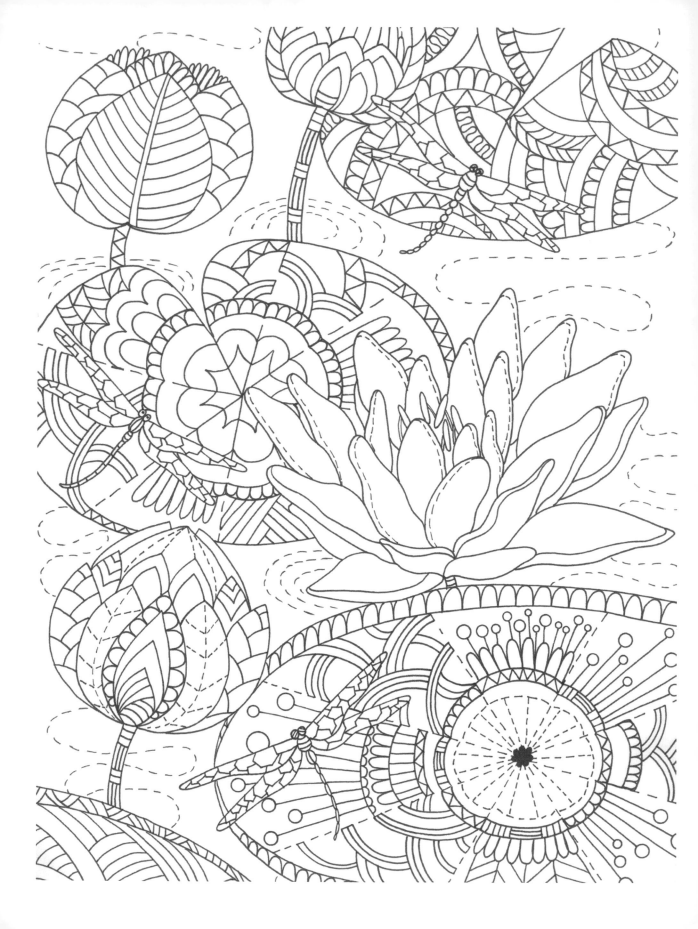

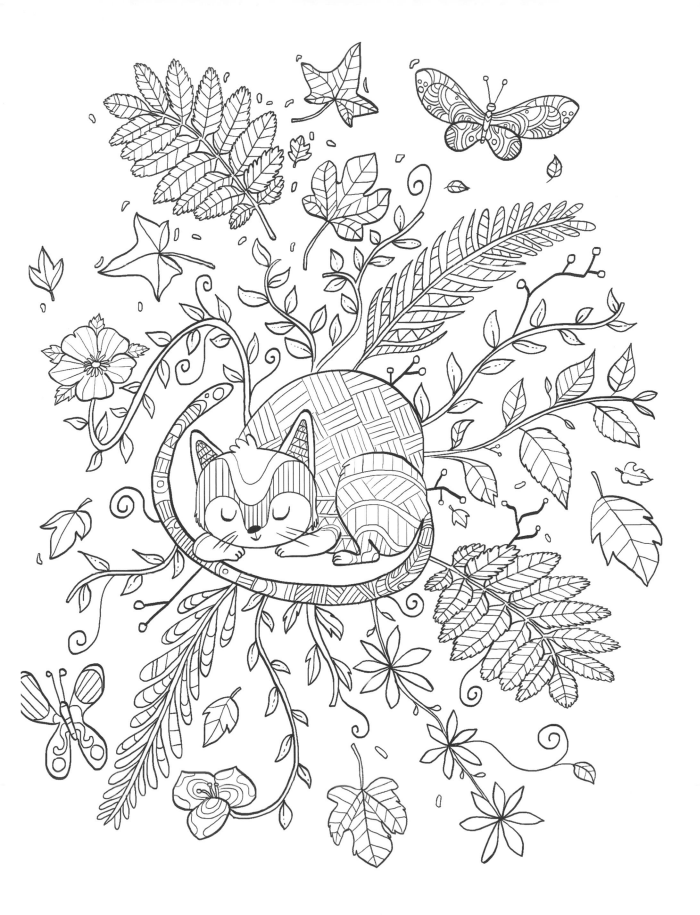

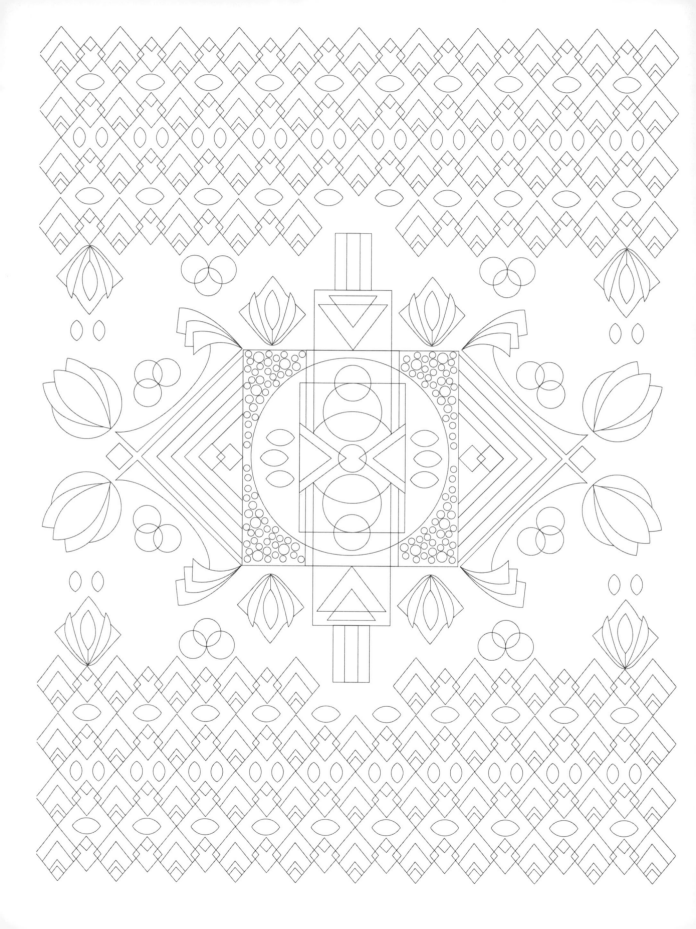

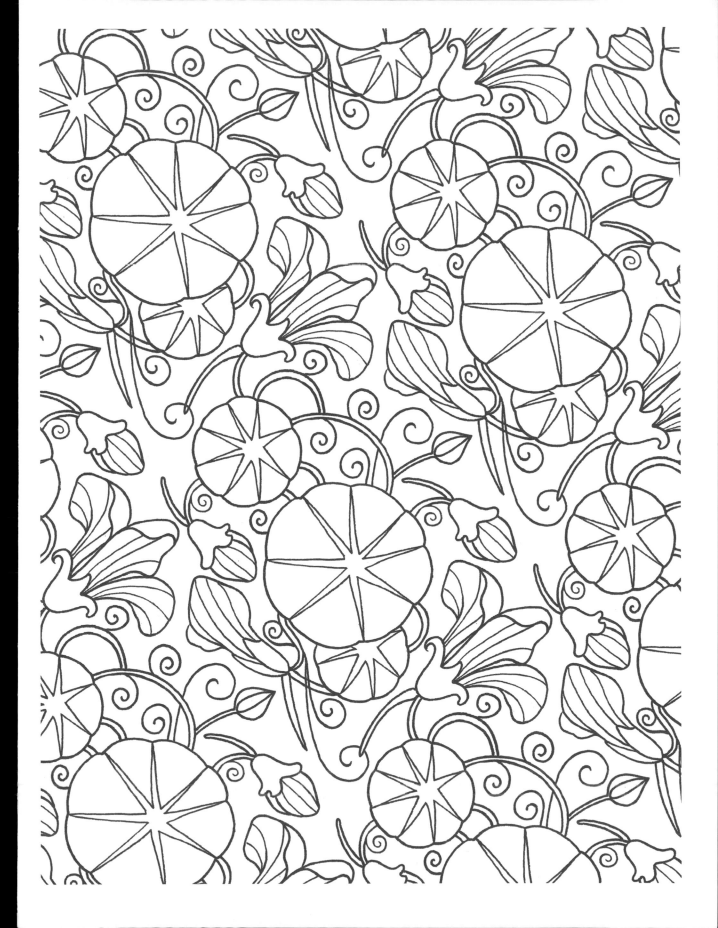

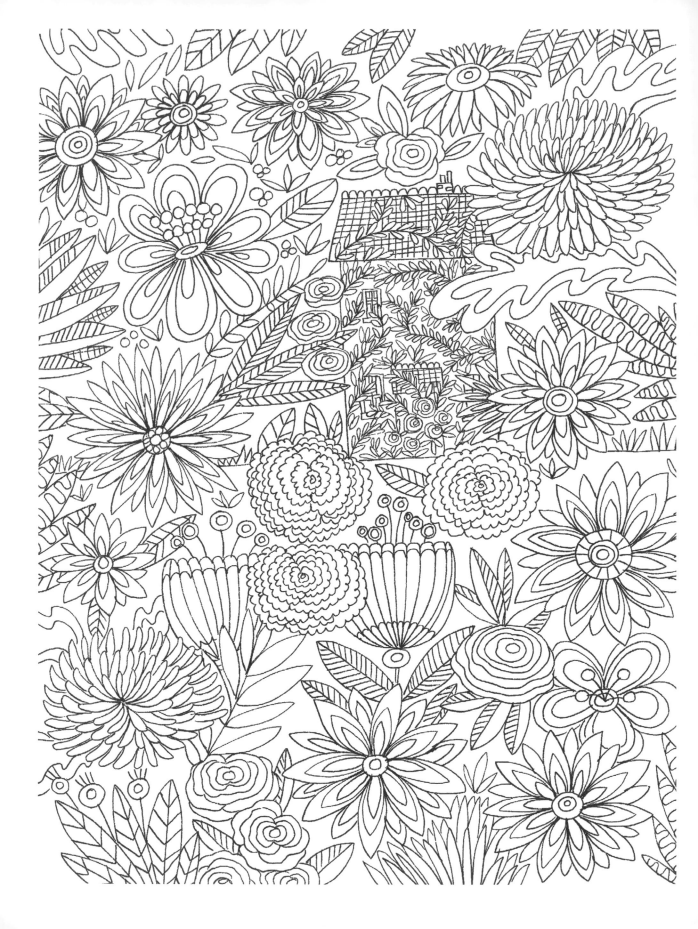

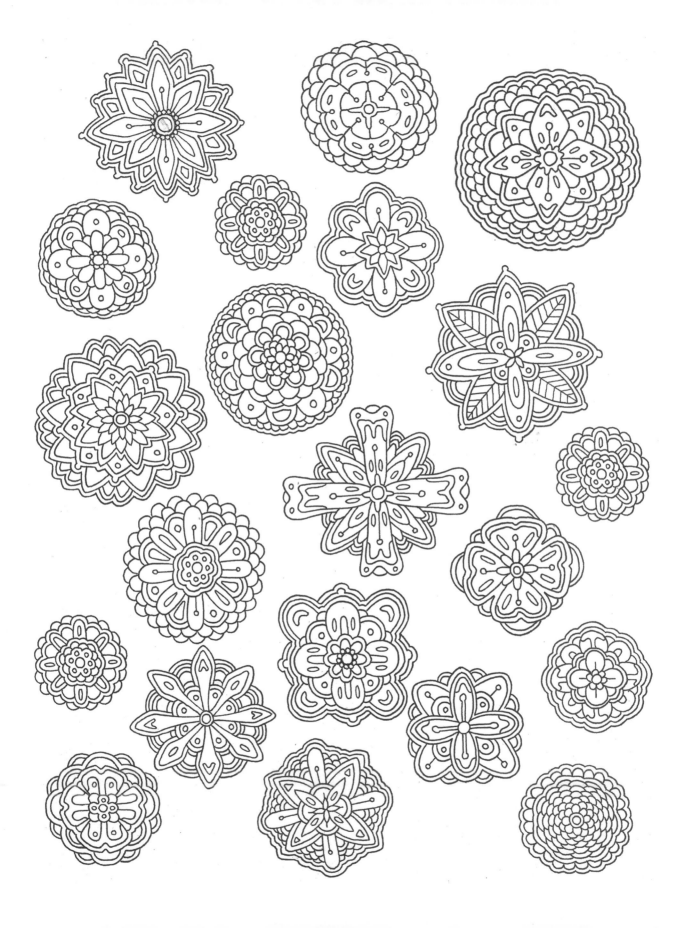

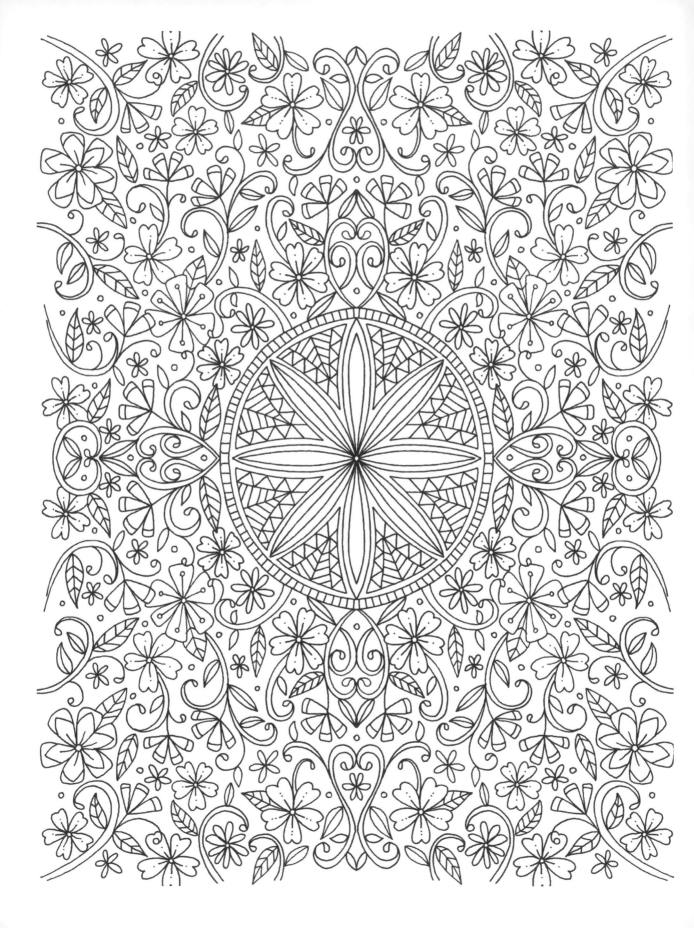

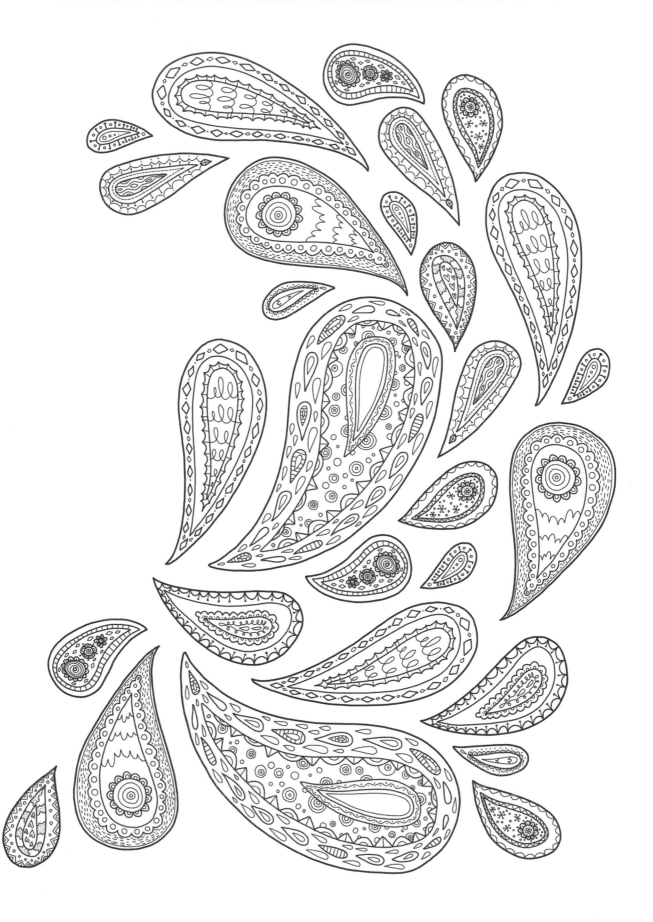

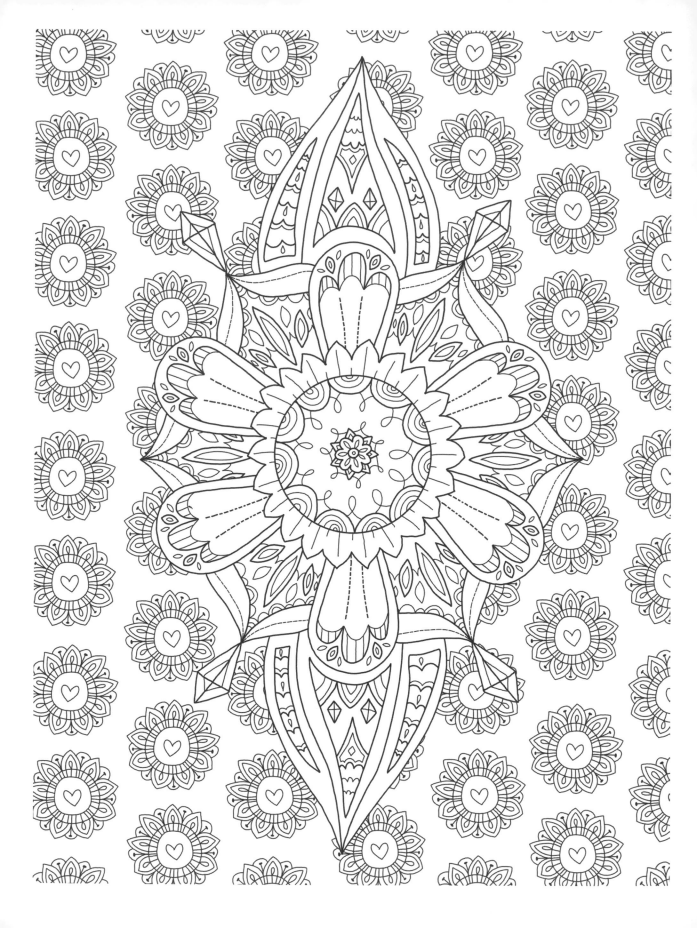

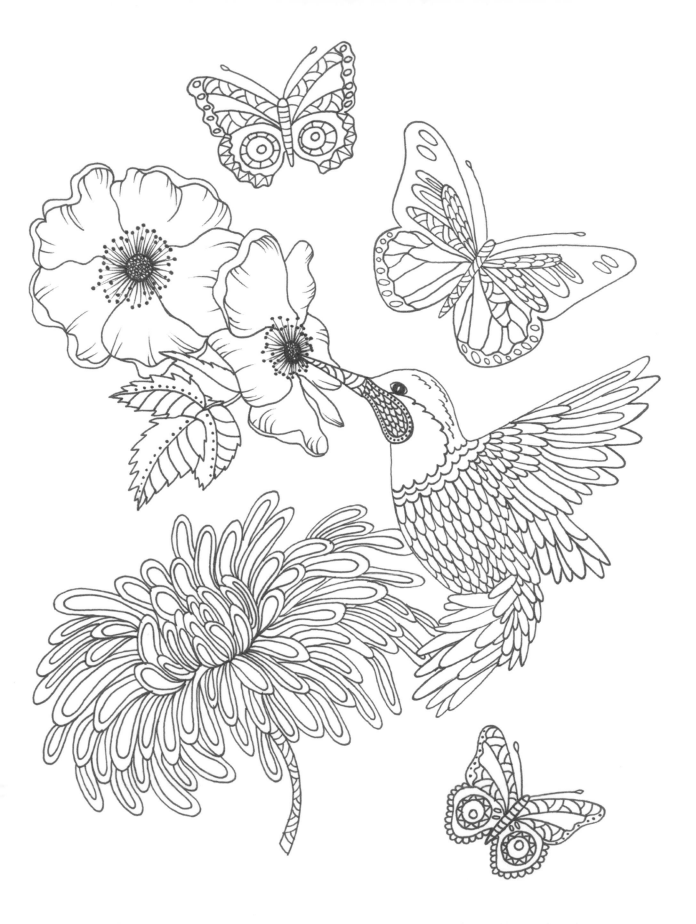

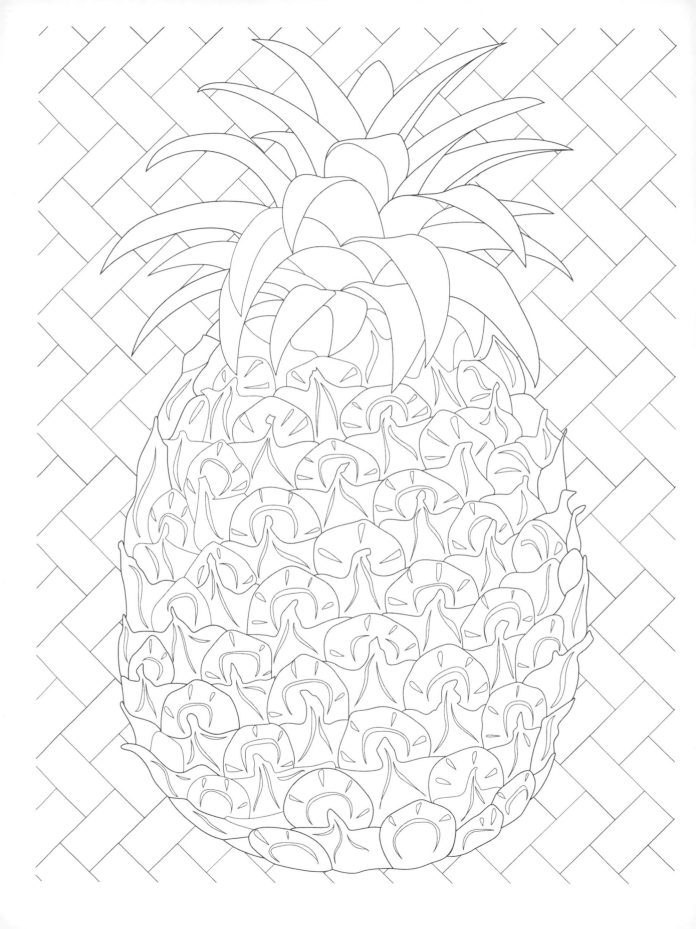

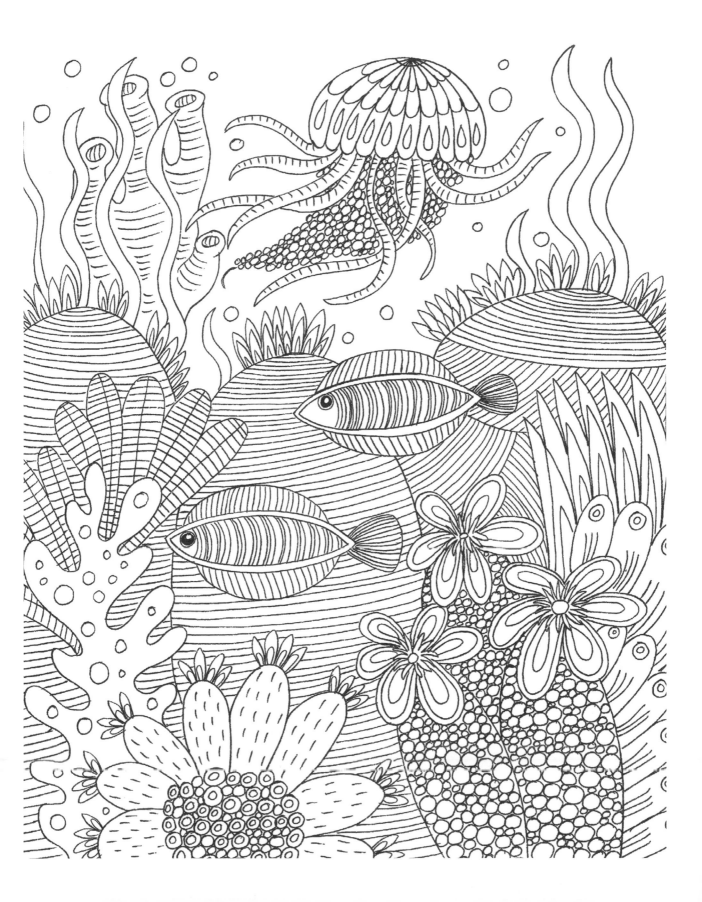

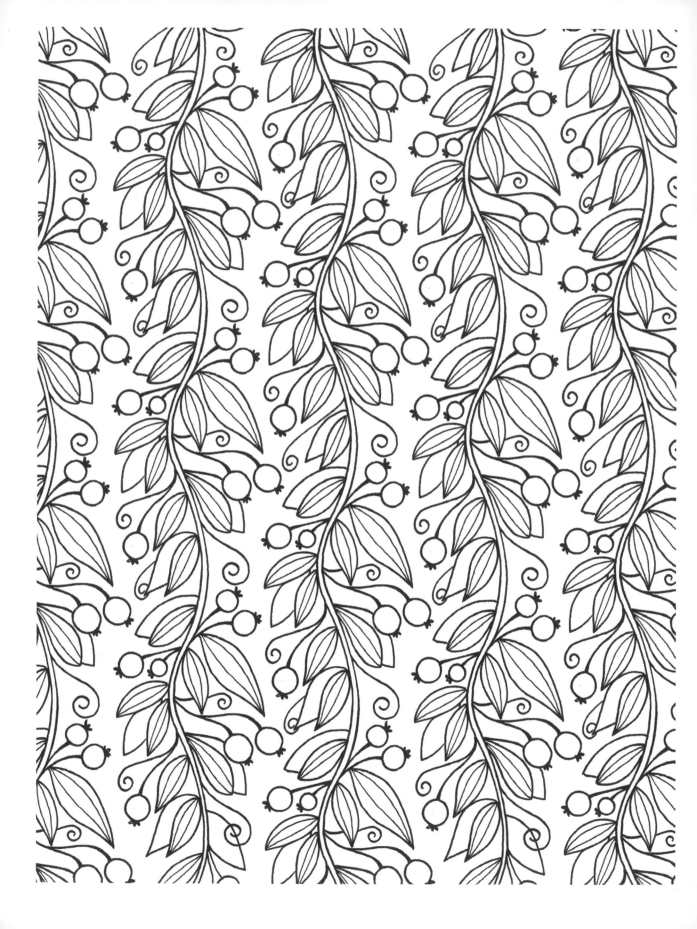

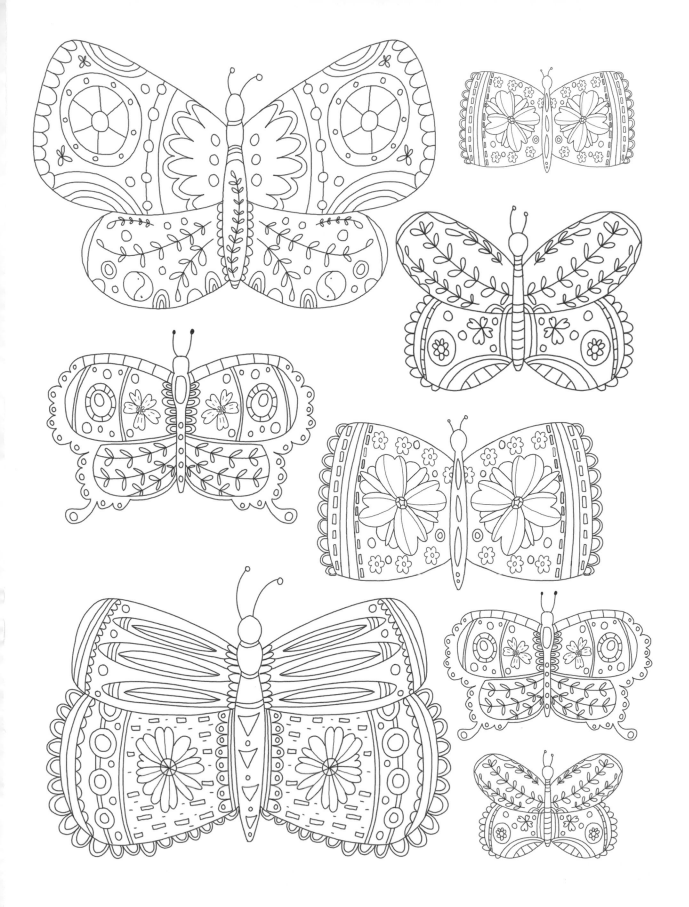

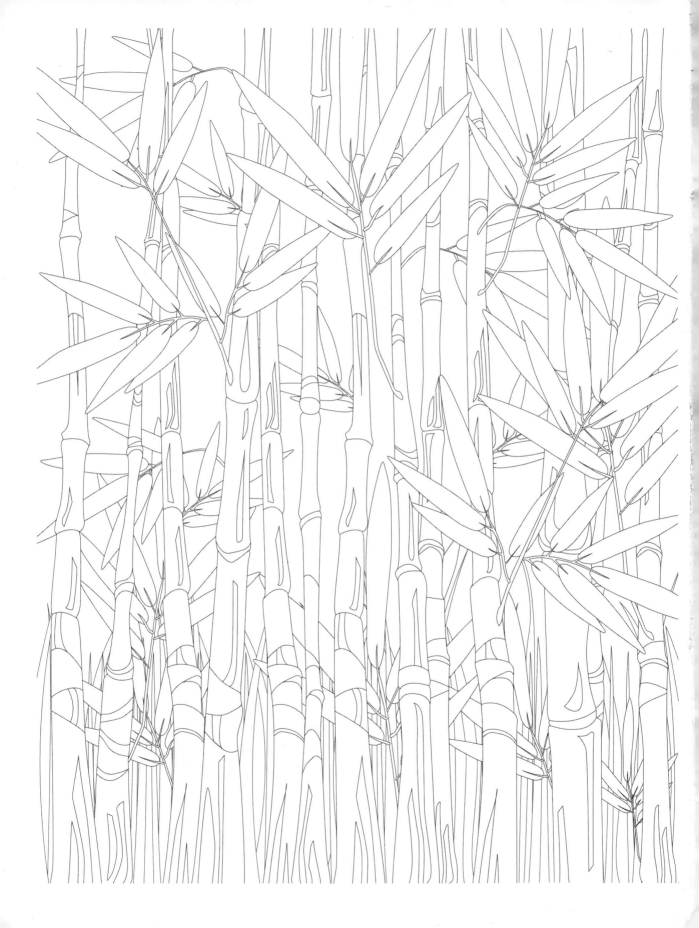